GIFTS OF SIGHT

DISCOVERING GOD'S LOVE THROUGH THE
LENS OF VISUAL IMPAIRMENT

KRISTIN GAULT

ABOVE THE
SUN

Published by Above The Sun, LLC

Cover Designed by Get Covers

This book has been produced in association with Above The Sun, LLC that has a mission to help authors release heaven through their authentic stories. For author coaching or publishing advice, learn more at https://abovethesun.org.

ENDORSEMENTS

In Gifts of Sight, I love how beautifully Kristin Gault bridges the gap between head knowledge and life experience which makes this book a captivating journey from start to finish. This is a must-read for anyone who is hungry for a fresh perspective on identity and ready to embark on a deeper quest of what it means to see and be seen, to know and be known by a loving God. So grab a copy and share with friends. You will not be disappointed!

~ **Lindsay Coil** – Speaker, Mentor, and Leadership Coach
Coil Coaching & Coil Coaching Women

~

Kristin Gault became a teacher to the visually impaired – but I've found, to some degree, we're *all* visually impaired – *spiritually*! Her revolutionary discoveries in bridging pathways of communication with children with disabilities correlate so wondrously with our human ability to *communicate with* God.

As Kristin candidly shares out of her personal experiences, she brings the reader along on a journey of revelation, healing, freedom, and new-found purpose. Throughout the pages of this book, God *has opened my eyes* to realize the limits inherently put on my own abilities to *see* and *hear* Him. With an open heart and mind, any reader is sure to be led by the Holy Spirit into the deeper waters of self-discovery and God-discovery, into a fuller, more beautiful, and exhilarating understanding of God's heart.

~ **Deb Allen** – Writer, graduate summa cum laude of the University of Oregon School of Journalism, 47-year follower of Christ.

~

Kristin Gault's book bears the mark of having been lived through. Her voice is authentic. She creatively integrates perspectives from her profession of working with visually impaired children and stories from her own faith journey, arriving at profound insights for life as followers of Jesus. The passion behind the book is Kristin's longing to help people see God as the loving Father he is and to see themselves in the light of that love. Knowing that God sees us as the person he created us to be and that his healing work helps us become that person doesn't just encourage. It transforms. This is a book that will change you.

~ **Nancy Thomas** – Poet, professor, pastor, and author of numerous books of poetry, biblical studies, and essays on ordinary grace.

~

Kristin, along with several other friends from our support group, decided to drive to the beach one weekend. We had such fun hunting for agates in the sand. Kristin is an expert at finding these beautiful, broken, shiny treasures unseen by the majority of people. My small pile didn't compare with the abundance of broken agates her trained eyes found that day.

The pile of colorful agates on the cover of her book speaks of Kristin's heart of compassion for broken people. Her heart is stirred for the visually disabled who are often unnoticed. She has a deep desire to let them know they are seen and loved. Your heart will melt as you read touching stories about how she does that in such innovative ways.

Kristin has two sons who are visually impaired. The diagnosis of her sons resulted in her decision to earn her degree in teaching others with this disability. While reading Kristin's book I felt like I was sitting in her classroom hanging on to her every word. She is such a great teacher. Vision is a complex system occurring inside the brain. The way Kristin describes this process is brilliant and understandable. Her writing held me captive from the beginning to the end.

Cortical Visual Impairment (CVI). is Kristin's area of expertise. This is a diagnosis where a person is blind as a result of a trauma to the brain. Kristin's obvious knowledge of how vision works and love for her treasured students shines through her book.

This book is for anyone who has ever felt unseen. I was reminded of the basic human need to be known and loved. You will be inspired in your faith by Kristin's continual correlation between CVI and biblical truths. These revelatory truths will remind you that just as Kristin seeks to help the broken see, God seeks us, desiring to unveil the eyes of our heart to see His love.

~ **Andi Smith** - Friend, music teacher, worship leader, author of Church Without Walls, contributor to Our Daily Bread, The Secret Place, God's Abundance for Women by Kathy Collard Miller, What's in the Bible for Couples by Kathy Collard Miller and D. Larry Miller, Encountering Angels by Judith MacNutt.

~

Gifts of Sight is a beautiful and inspiring work that reveals the profound depths of God's love through the lens of visual impairment. Kristin Gault takes readers on a deeply moving journey, one that unveils spiritual truths within the challenges of disability. This book is a captivating exploration of how our most profound gifts are often found in what the world perceives as brokenness. Gault's insights create a spiritual hunger within the reader's soul, beckoning us to embrace a reality where every limitation contains a blessed invitation to experience the boundless love of the Creator.

~ **Elisheba Haxby** – Speaker, Mentor, and Author of the Ninety-Nine Series.

This book is dedicated to my friend, Jess.
Your friendship has played a significant role in encouraging
me to grow into my true identity.
I see now that God placed you in my life at the perfect time.
You will always have a special place in my heart.

Those who sow their tears as seeds
will reap a harvest with joyful shouts of glee.
(Psalm 126:5 TPT)

You prepare a table before me in the presence of my enemies; you anoint my
head with oil, my cup overflows.
(Psalm 23:5 CSB)

CONTENTS

FORWARD

Kristin asked me to write a foreword for a book about visual impairment that would correlate with our spiritual journey. Quite frankly, I wasn't interested in this topic. Visual impairment and all the technical, scientific, and therapeutic knowledge needed to understand this specific field felt very daunting. But I immediately agreed to take the time to read her book and write a foreword once she was completed. Why? Over the years I have known Kristin, I have watched her transform into a confident and bold woman of faith who brought great encouragement and value to those around her.

As often happens with busy individuals, I didn't get around to reading her manuscript until there was a firm deadline. Once I started reading, I was immediately captivated. As a person who firmly believes that God's creation has cohesion and correlation and that holistic health is His heart's desire for all His children, it was fascinating to read how Kristin mined the physiology of visual impairment to gain emotional and spiritual insights. As an avid reader of spiritual revelation, I am astounded by the level of original revelation Kristin shares in this book. Yet, the originality of her insights is married to very practical applications in our journey of faith.

Within these pages, you'll discover a unique blend of science, teaching principles, personal encounters, practical application, and bold discussions of the supernatural. While many books delve into personal supernatural experiences, it's rare to find one that fearlessly explores the supernatural alongside scientific explanations. This distinctive approach is a testament to Kristin's originality and her commitment to providing a comprehensive understanding of her subject matter.

Personally, I was rather startled by how many of her deep encounters with the Lord happened during our conferences. To be asked to write an endorsement for one of our regular attendees who found radical freedom through hunger and personal pursuit of the Lord is an honor that words cannot adequately express. I am so grateful that I had to read this book to follow through with my commitment. I believe this book has multiple functions. One can read to garner knowledge about this specific field. A parent of a special needs child can find great encouragement that there are dedicated professionals who will love their child and foster healing. And those looking for a daily devotional book that can add spiritual insights into their own Spirit-filled journey of faith will find practical tools to enhance their journey.

I will purchase several copies of Kristin's book to give away as gifts once it is published. Her work is truly a gift to Christians and non-Christians alike. I know you will be blessed as you read because Kristin's honesty and authenticity will embolden you to look for God's fingerprint in your life.

Soorin Backer

Soorin Backer Ministries

Founder and Senior Leader of Thrive Movement Church

NABI Medial Productions Studio

INTRODUCTION

"Come away, my lover. Come with me to the faraway fields. We will run away together to the forgotten places and show them redeeming love."
(Song of Songs 7:11 TPT)

A stick here. A rock there. Sometimes a random leaf. Each one lying all by itself on the ground, seemingly forgotten. They ended up being taken to my room to a special spot under my bed.

I have always had a heart for those who have been forgotten, even for inanimate objects. When I was a kid growing up in La Paz, Bolivia, I had lots of sticks, stones, and leaves under my bed. I would find a stone all by itself and feel bad for it. I would pick it up and bring it home. The same with twigs and leaves.

When I first came across this verse in Song of Songs as an adult, it spoke to me. Forgotten places... Forgotten things. This is what I'd always wanted to do—to find people who experienced being forgotten and passed over and show them God's redeeming love. Show them they are valued and noticed.

Most people have felt unvalued and unimportant at some point in their lives. Overlooked. Forgotten. Some of us have bought into these lies and allowed them to influence how we view ourselves. Because we have believed that we are not worthy, there is an assumption others also think of us this way. Many of us have this desperate need to be known. A desperate need to be seen and loved.

The truth is we have a God who sees each one of us. A God who understands our actions and thoughts wholly. A God who loves completely without reservation. This truth is woven throughout the Scriptures starting in Genesis 16:13. Hagar has run away from her life circumstances. Feeling alone and lost, she encounters God and comes away from that encounter forever changed. The name given to God here is El Roi, Hebrew for "The God Who Sees."

David wrote in Psalms, "Your eyes saw me when I was formless; all my days were written in your book and planned before a single one of them began" (Psalm 139:16 CSB). We have a God who sees, knows, and loves. Unconditionally. I say this because I live it, both as a recipient as well as a provider.

When our firstborn, Reilly, was a baby, he was diagnosed with a visual impairment, but we received little information regarding it. It was only after our third child, Peter was born around five years later that we learned more about both boys.

Peter was an easy baby—a little too easy. He did all the things he was supposed to do physically but didn't respond to us. He didn't respond to his name being called, didn't turn his head towards us, and was unresponsive in other ways. He did laugh at being tickled, so we attributed his behavior to his personality.

Right before we had to take Peter in for his three-month check-up, the Bible story was brought to my mind about the man whose blindness was presumed to be a result of sin. Jesus's response to this accusation was that no one in his family sinned to cause his blindness, but it was rather that God's works would be displayed in him (see John 9:1-3). God highlighted this story to me on two different occasions before this appointment. At the time I didn't understand the reason or timing for this.

Two days after Peter's check-up we were told by an ophthalmologist that Peter only had light perception and was basically blind. He was diagnosed with optic nerve hypoplasia, which is a condition where the optic nerve is underdeveloped and complications with the pituitary gland are likely. We were in shock. It never occurred to us that Peter was blind. His eyes looked perfectly fine, other than the fact that they moved constantly like Reilly's.

It's funny how God works in unexpected circumstances. What happened next is one of the first times I sensed being *seen* and *loved* by God. Shortly after the diagnosis, I was approached by a well-respected older woman during a church potluck. She asked what sins my husband and I had not dealt with because she believed Peter was blind as a result of our sin. Immediately, I remembered the passage I had read in John 9:1-3 a few days earlier. God had highlighted it to me not once but twice right before Peter's diagnosis. Something supernatural took place inside of me at that moment. Instead of experiencing anger and disbelief at the woman's accusation, I felt so much joy and peace because I knew God loved me. He knew this was going to happen and so prepared me. Through this circumstance, God showed me personally He held our lives in His capable and loving hands and that I need not question why my boys were visually impaired.

As is often the case with optic nerve hypoplasia, Peter's vision gradually continued to develop after his first year, and he is now considered low vision. We learned about Reilly's vision through our experience with Peter. Both boys were diagnosed with the same condition along with oculocutaneous albinism. Peter's pituitary gland ended up not being affected, but he was diagnosed with autism at an early age.

Because of my boys, I was led to go back to school to become a Teacher for the Visually Impaired (TVI). In my job, I was drawn to the area of cortical/cerebral visual impairment (CVI). I saw that the students who had this diagnosis tended to be the ones who fell through the cracks and received the least amount of services. Those most easily forgotten.

Interestingly enough, becoming a teacher was not my primary reason for going to college. My bachelor's degree was in Sociology/Social Work. However, I discovered my love for teaching while living overseas with my husband. I loved teaching, but through a string of unexpected events, God again changed the trajectory of my life.

To be seen is one of the most important aspects of life for all of us. To see is just as important a calling as being the hands and feet of Jesus. We are also called to be His eyes. I want to be known as one who sees through His eyes and loves accordingly.

This book is about my own journey into wholeness, including my experience working with and loving my students with a focus on CVI, and how this serves as an analogy to show God's love for us.

To see and be seen. To know and be known.

Searching for Agates

Those who know me recognize I have a thing for agates. For me, agates represent unexpected blessings. I particularly like to collect the small agates that are broken. They are like the fractured pieces of our lives, those things that did not go as we expected, those things that hurt and scarred us. They become beautiful as light shines through them. They remind me of how God can take everything that happens and bring good out of it if we let Him. This book is full of agates God has given me.

It was last summer right before I started writing this book when my husband and I were spending a few days on the coast. I went on a walk by myself along the beach looking for agates early one morning, just talking with God. On this walk, I found the most beautiful agates, including a purple heart stone. I sensed God wanting me to give these agates back to Him by placing them in a pile on a big rock. It was to be a gift to pass on for someone else. I felt permission to keep the purple heart for remembrance sake. The picture on the front of this book show those agates, including the purple heart I found.

My prayer as you read this book is that if you search, you will be able to perceive the agates in your own life. Many of the discoveries in this book came through my job and delving deep into the area of cortical/cerebral visual impairment. Through the lens of CVI, I've seen many correlations between my experience with CVI and my own journey with God. My hope is that, as I share my story of discovering how I am seen and known by God, you'll understand that you are seen and known too, and how that leads to a new vision of the person God created you to be. A new identity.

If you have ever felt abandoned, alone, forgotten, or unseen, this book is for you. Maybe your story is not about having a child with a disability. It can be about anything. For many of us, life has not gone as we planned it. It could involve a difficult childhood, a job loss, a divorce, an unexpected move, the death of a loved one... Through it all, God knows. God is aware of every detail of your life. And cares. Deeply.

These truths are not just for me but for all who follow the Lord. God wants to work through you, and I believe He has an incredible future in store for each of us. A future we cannot even imagine. He is able to do exceedingly abundantly beyond all that we ask or think. If you are at a place where your faith is weak, take comfort in the fact that God recognizes that, and He will continue to work in your life if you allow Him to. I am confident after reading this book that you will start recognizing all the agates God has given you. Searching and finding them is part of the journey of growing into a deeper relationship with God.

"We know that all things work together for the good of those who love God, who are called according to his purpose." (Romans 8:28 CSB)

Disclaimer

No theological or scientific claims are being made in this book. This is me speaking about my life and how I view it through the lens of CVI. All references of The CVI Range pertaining to Dr. Roman-Lantzy or any other professional do not reflect their views in this book.

PART I

UNDERSTANDING VISION

1

PAYING ATTENTION

"But blessed are your eyes because they see,
and your ears because they hear." (Matthew 13:16 NIV)

Every Thursday after work, I meet with a group of close friends. On one particular afternoon, I was on my way to the group when a van ignored the stop sign and drove right into my path. I braced myself for impact when I sensed the car being lifted up and placed safely on the side of the road, out of the path of the van. I sat for the next few minutes shaking after the van had driven off. There was no explanation for what had happened.

I had another incident where I was driving home from the office on Highway 99. A truck ahead of me was carrying long boards of plywood in the back. I noticed they were not secured. I watched in horror as one wiggled loose and headed straight for my windshield. Then somehow it was "lifted" above my car, landing safely on the side of the road behind me.

Both episodes got my attention to say the least. I could not deny that God had stepped in and protected me. All I could think of was that God had plans for me and it was not yet my time.

3

During this time of my life, I was learning who God was. I had a relationship with Him but felt like I was only scratching the surface, not sure how to get deeper. God was beckoning me to come closer. I desired to share every aspect of my life with Him, not just go to church on Sundays and have a little bit of quiet time during the week. I longed to live life with Him. All of it. My hunger to know God was growing, and I desperately wanted to recognize His voice in my life. Thus began what I call my "pin-point obedience" adventure.

To me, pin-point obedience is the practice of learning to listen, hear, and then obey God's voice. It involves fine-tuning one's ability to recognize God's voice by listening to every nudge or whisper that comes to mind and acting on it. Through it, I learned to be more attentive, and my awareness of God working in my life grew. More often than not, I learned that these random thoughts that would enter my brain were from God, whether it was to give an encouraging word to a friend, send a text, or sometimes approach a stranger in the store. The correlation between purposeful attentiveness to hear from God resulting in obedience was made very clear to me in the fall of 2022.

I was getting ready to go to a conference led by Soorin Backer when a friend sent me a text. She had been praying for me and was impressed with a vision that came to mind regarding this particular conference. What she saw was a burning bush in front of me. My friend believed that this would be a time when God and I would get so close one wouldn't be able to tell where one began and the other ended. Within the first thirty seconds of the conference starting, the speaker highlighted the burning bush from the story of Moses. It felt more than coincidental; God had my full attention.

God still gives His people the prophetic ability to have visions or words for others in order to encourage them (see 1 Corinthians 14:3). Another friend recently shared the verse from Habakkuk 2:1 (NIV): "I will stand my watch... I will look to see what the Lord will say to me." There are times when the things of God, the spiritual, are so very often too deep for words. In these times, God uses visions as a way to communicate with us.

The burning bush symbolizes to me God's desire to turn our eyes towards Him so we can walk in close relationship with Him. Moses had many doubts about his ability to do what God had instructed him to do. He stuttered and couldn't speak in front of people. He didn't see himself as able to lead God's people out of Egypt. This encounter with the burning bush started the process of removing his fears and unwillingness to step out. In the same way, at this conference, I felt my fears begin to diminish as my desire to grow close to God was greater. He was preparing me for what He was calling me to do: to show others they are seen and, in turn, to help them see.

On the drive home, two events transpired. The first involved stopping at the house of a close friend of someone in our group who had been suffering from a degenerative neurological disease. As a result of this condition, she had lost much motor movement and had been in a wheelchair for many years with limited exposure to the world outside and few visitors, living largely unseen. She had been experiencing intense physical pain throughout her body, where nerves would fire off randomly turning into excruciatingly painful spasms. This could happen several times an hour throughout a day, while other days there may be only three to four episodes. There wasn't a rhyme or reason to where or when the pain would target her body. Fear became a daily companion for two years as she never knew how the pain would manifest itself in the day ahead. She needed a touch from God, an acknowledgement that she mattered and was not forgotten.

As the four of us laid hands on this dear friend and began to pray and call out to God, healing was released. The physical pain completely went away, and the spasms stopped. These last two years she has still not had a single episode to this day. The way God showed up demonstrated His love for this woman. She was His daughter, deeply loved!

Right after this visit, I sensed a strong nudge to go visit a friend who was going through a dark time in her life. This is someone I care about deeply and had been praying for. I had to battle fear in my heart for what I was being led to do as I didn't know what her reaction would be to me coming over and praying with her. I stepped out in faith, and what followed was something neither one of us could have anticipated. God's love for her overwhelmed me in a way I had never experienced before. As this love poured through me a deep emotional healing took place in her. I had the privilege of being a part of it simply because I had placed myself in a position to not only hear from God, but to obey despite feelings of inadequacy and fear.

I have heard it said that out of all the nudges we may get, it is better to listen and obey one hundred percent of the time and be right half the time. The other option is to listen sometimes or not at all, missing out on opportunities God places in our lives. These are opportunities to hear what He has to say to us as well as opportunities to show His love for others. If I had not positioned myself to pay attention to the "burning bush", I would have missed out on being a part of God's healing plan to touch these friends.

Getting Our Attention

As an analogy, the first part of this book will address the beginning processes of vision in the brain. I like to think of this part of vision as a four piece puzzle. Each piece needs to be present in order for the puzzle to make sense. The first, and arguably most important piece to vision, is attention.

In Exodus, we read the story about Moses and how he was tending his father-in-law's flock when he came upon this burning bush. What strikes me about this story is that Moses stopped when he saw the burning bush and he *chose to go over*. He was paying attention and took time to delve further into what was happening. He could have kept on walking and missed this opportunity to hear God speak. But because he turned aside, he stepped into a divine encounter with God. God had his attention, and he had God's attention (see Exodus 3:1-4).

Another attention grabbing moment from the Bible was with Paul. Paul was a man of great focus, but before his conversion moment, he was as spiritually blind as one could be. He was known for persecuting those who believed in Jesus. In the first verse of Acts 9, Paul, previously known as Saul, is described as one full of anger and rage towards Christians. Various translations describe him as being "eager to kill" and wanting to "murder" anyone who fell into this category. Saul even went so far as to get special permission to intentionally find anyone who believed in Jesus, men and women, to arrest them and put them in prison. He wasn't about to be persuaded and listen to reason from any man, but God got his attention in a drastic way.

Verses 3-4 (TPT) describe what happened to Saul who was on his way to Damascus with the sole purpose of arresting these Jesus followers: "So, he obtained the authorization and left for Damascus. Just outside the city, a brilliant light flashing from heaven suddenly exploded all around him. Falling to the ground, he heard a booming voice say to him, 'Saul, Saul, why are you persecuting me?'" God continued to talk to him, instructing him what to do next. Saul was physically blind for three days and did not eat or drink. Through this course of action, God gained Saul's attention, which led to his transformation. Fortunately for us, this is not the typical method God uses.

Further on in the same chapter is another example of how God gets our attention. In verse 10, God gives a vision to a man named Ananias. "Living in Damascus was a believer named Ananias. The Lord spoke to him in a vision, calling his name, 'Ananias.' 'Yes, Lord,' Ananias answered." It seems like Ananias was intentionally living in a posture of paying attention and being alert for whenever the Lord spoke to him.

When God had Ananias' attention, they had a conversation about him going to meet Saul, ending with Ananias demonstrating that pinpoint obedience to God's direction was vital, even when it went against all reason. The Lord told him to go meet Saul who had been struck blind and to restore his vision. God directed him to show mercy to this man who was persecuting all those who believed in Jesus. Because Ananias was paying attention to God, he was able to recognize God's voice and obey despite experiencing fear. His attention was more tuned into what God was saying than what the world was telling him. The result of his paying attention to God was the beginning of Saul's conversion. Referred to as Paul from then on, he went to spread the Good News of Jesus throughout the land.

Where to Direct Our Attention

The truth is, we have an enemy who also vies for our attention. Satan wants to distract us. The definition of distraction is the thing that prevents someone from giving full attention to something else. Satan recognizes that whatever we give our attention to, that is where we place our hope, desire, and faith. For this reason, Paul commands us in the book of Philippians to "Keep your thoughts continually fixed on all that is authentic and real, honorable and admirable, beautiful and respectful, pure and holy, merciful and kind. And fasten your thoughts on every glorious work of God, praising him always" (Philippians 4:8 TPT). We need to focus, to place our attention on what is true.

Jesus shares the parable of the seeds to address this. "Then he told them many things in parables, saying, 'A farmer went out to sow his seed. As he was scattering the seed, some fell along the path, and the birds came and ate it up. Some fell on rocky places, where it did not have much soil. It sprang up quickly, because the soil was shallow. But when the sun came up, the plants were scorched and withered because they had no root. Other seed fell among thorns, which grew up and choked the plants. Still other seed fell on good soil, where it produced a crop - a hundred, sixty, or thirty times what was sown. Whoever has ears, let them hear'" (Matthew 13:3-9 NIV).

The birds, rocks, shallow soil, and thorns allude to what distracts us from focusing on what is true. We may hear the Good News, but then the distractions of life, including the lies we have bought into, take our attention away from the truth. When we plant seeds and water them, weeds may spring up alongside the plant that was intentionally planted. These weeds can represent fear and doubt that tend to creep in when we perceive God speaking to us. We have to be intentional about pulling out those weeds so we can keep our focus on what was planted in us. We have to refuse to let those weeds distract us. If we keep tending the seed of His truth, that which is authentic and real, it will grow and bloom in time. That one seed has the potential to grow into a bush or a tree. Maybe even thousands of trees if tended properly.

What Impares Our Vision

Many people do not understand the full process of how vision works, and to be fair, neither did I until I entered my field of study. It is a common assumption to believe vision only takes place in the eyes, but as neuroscientist David Engelman likes to point out, the visual system is much more complex than a simple camera. Many may think vision is equal to our other senses, but the truth is, out of all our senses, vision is the most dominant. There are studies that say 40-50% of our brain is dedicated to our visual processes. To put this into perspective, the auditory sense only uses 3% of our brain while the tactile sense uses around 10%.

Unfortunately, there are times when the visual information coming in cannot be interpreted accurately. Nothing may be wrong physically with the eyes, but the brain has somehow failed to receive and understand what one may be looking at. A disruption in the process has occurred.

Cortical/cerebral visual impairment (CVI) is a diagnosis where the visual processing areas of the brain are impacted at some level. The individual has difficulty interpreting what their eyes may be directed towards or fixated on. CVI is a result of trauma to the brain, whether this be congenital or acquired later in life.

CVI has now become the most common cause for visual impairment worldwide as well as the least understood and the most undiagnosed. It is believed that for every student who has been diagnosed with CVI, there are four more who have not yet been identified. Because the brain is so involved, other challenges often exist that contribute to the misunderstanding of students with CVI. These additional challenges can include the inability to communicate verbally, the inability to move one's limbs, difficulty with cognitive tasks, being prone to seizures, etc. Adding these extra challenges to a lack of understanding regarding the brain's involvement in vision has contributed to the lack and level of intervention needed.

There are several methods used to assess someone who is diagnosed with CVI. For the purposes of this book, I will be referring to the CVI Range Assessment by Dr. Christine Roman-Lantzy. In this assessment, Dr. Roman groups individuals into three phases.

The first phase, known as Phase I, includes those individuals who have very little visual response. They are not able to see and understand most of what is in their world. Their eyes may be open, but their gaze appears empty, not staring or fixated purposefully on anything. However, some level of visual ability is almost always present, and intervention is based on this. The goal in this phase is to build visual awareness by creating neural pathways in the brain where this small level of vision can be processed. As the individual progresses in their visual skills, the hope is they move into the later phases.

I have learned two main things in my journey working with students with this type of visual impairment: 1) some degree of vision is always present in an individual with this condition, and 2) CVI is complex. Each child is unique, and there is no one size fits all approach. Intervention for each student needs to be carefully thought out and takes time.

Building Awareness

Are you aware of how God gets your attention?

The first puzzle piece of vision that needs to be present for this process to start is the ability to pay attention. People need to have the capacity to be attentive and alert. An individual who is able to be attentive enough to focus on something will greatly increase their ability to process what they are looking at. The same concept can be applied for us as people and how we experience God.

I once heard a story about two people walking down a street in New York. There was a lot of noise. Suddenly, one of the men stopped and asked the other, "Can you hear that?" His friend said, "Hear what?" Noise was all around. Traffic, cars honking, construction, people talking. The man who stopped said, "It's a cricket!" His friend was amazed that he could attend to this tiny sound amidst all the chaotic city noise.

The point is, the man who noticed the noise was one who studies insects. He had spent his life paying attention to insects. He had extensive knowledge, including what sounds they each made. In the same way, the more we spend time with Jesus, the easier it is to recognize Him in others, even others different than ourselves, and the more easily we can recognize Him in the midst of all the noise and chaos life brings.

Are you making a conscious effort to pay attention? We don't read much about Ananias except for these few verses in the Bible, but he must have been well acquainted with God's voice to recognize it that quickly—a testament to the time spent listening to God.

Another example found in the Bible is when God first called out to a young boy named Samuel, who later became a mighty prophet for God. Initially, God had to call Samuel multiple times before he recognized who was calling him (see I Samuel 3:4-8). God didn't stop trying to get his attention. Once God got Samuel's attention, Samuel spent his life paying attention to His voice.

What distractions are present in your life, pulling you away from living focused on God? The distractions may not be anything obvious, but more subtle. I have heard it said that most of us live our lives on autopilot. Life has a way of taking more and more of our conscious attention, and by the time we are adults most of us only give a small amount of conscious attention to our day to day experience. We may have lived more consciously when we fell in love, and everything we did was with that special person in mind. What would they think if I did this, wore that, said such and such... What if we were so in love with God that we lived our lives intentionally conscious of all we did in the light of Him?

The incredible thing in all of this is that we have a God who understands us to the core just as He understood Saul. A God whose ability to speak to us is greater than our ability to hear. A God who wants our attention so we can recognize Him unquestionably. A God who doesn't give up on us. A God who wants us to discover Him more than we could ever imagine.

We have a God whose ability to speak to us is greater than our ability to hear.

"I pray that the God of our Lord Jesus Christ, the glorious Father, would give you the Spirit of wisdom and revelation in the knowledge of him" (Ephesians 1:17 CSB).

And because He comprehends us better than we comprehend ourselves, He knows how to break through our defenses so we can in turn perceive Him. He knows how to get our attention. He actively pursues us. The thing is, He gives us the choice of whether or not we will pay attention. Are we willing to let go of that which distracts us from God? If your heart is yearning for Him, rest in the knowledge that He will be faithful and will enable you to experience Him.

What if you have trouble believing in God? Saul did not believe in Jesus, yet God loved him so much that he went through drastic means to get his attention. When He does get our attention, it can be through a radical experience, like having your car moved out of the way of an oncoming van. Or God may try to get your attention in a more subtle way, like a thought coming into your brain.

One of my favorite devotional books is called *I Hear His Whisper* by Brian Simmons. God often speaks to us in whispers, thoughts, and nudges. I encourage you to start paying attention to those nudges in your spirit, those ideas that "pop" into your mind at random times, in dreams that occur at night that you remember. God tends to work like this.

God sees us, hears us, and knows us. He wants us to see, hear, and know him. We simply need to be paying attention.

2

THE ABILITY TO UNDERSTAND

"Open up my understanding to the ways of your wisdom..."
(Psalms 119:27 TPT)

Henry is a special student of mine. I first met him when he was in the 6th grade and had recently moved into our school district. Henry is in a wheelchair with limited mobility due to cerebral palsy. He is impacted by cortical visual impairment (CVI) and uses his vision in a very limited functional way. Henry is also nonverbal. The first time I worked with him, he was sitting by himself in a swing. I tried to have a conversation but didn't get much of a response back. I brainstormed ways to open up interaction with him and brought a kit I had put together. This kit later turned into my BaseKit for my VistaQuest business. Through spending time going through activities in the kit, I began to identify what got Henry's attention. Even though much of the time Henry still put his head down and closed his eyes, I sensed he was more aware of his surroundings than we realized. But I felt stuck in my ability to communicate with him.

My good friend and colleague, Amy, came alongside me and worked with Henry on using a communication system. Amy is a Speech and Language Pathologist as well as an Augmentative and Alternative

Communication Specialist. AAC is a type of communication that does not use verbal speech. Alternate methods such as using objects, symbols, gestures, signing, electronic devices, and communication books are examples of AAC.

Amy introduced Henry to a PODD system. PODD stands for Pragmatic Organization Dynamic Display. This is a system where symbols and words are organized to support and encourage communication. It can seem very daunting at first. However, as I used PODD with Henry, I found that it opened up communication in a way I did not think possible. I was able to ask him questions and model for him how to say yes or no by implementing his natural body movements. Gradually, we started to receive responses from Henry.

One day his physical therapist and I took him out into the hallway of the school to put him into a specialized tricycle so he could get some exercise. When it was time to transfer Henry back into his wheelchair, I noticed tears coming down his cheeks. Using the PODD system, he was able to tell me that he didn't understand what was happening next. We stopped what we were doing and helped him touch his wheelchair, explaining we were going to be moving him into it. Then we'd be going back to the classroom where it was time to eat. Henry's body relaxed, and he got a big smile on his face, signaling he understood. He was learning to communicate his feelings, realizing that he would be listened to.

Another time while coming to work with Henry, I noticed he had been listening to a story on his device. The previous week I had discovered most of the audiobooks were more appropriate for preschool-age students. Henry was a middle schooler, so I switched these out for more age-appropriate books. That day I had several activities to show Henry so we went to the back of the room where it was quieter and less chaotic. We were going to practice making choices with these activities. It was not the first time we had done this. However, on this particular day, I could get no response from him. Henry put his head down, covered his eyes, and would not respond.

Whenever I give a set of choices, I have learned to always include the option of "something different." Henry would not even choose that. I went through his PODD book trying to figure out what was wrong—still no response.

Finally, I bent down so I could look at his face and communicate what I thought he was feeling due to his body language. I said, "I see you putting your head down and closing your eyes, and this makes me think you are ignoring me, hoping I will go away so you can get back to listening to your book." A big grin appeared on Henry's face, and he started laughing. I loved it. His clear communication showed me he knew exactly what was going on and was ignoring me on purpose. The ability to understand as well as the realization that others can understand you when you communicate, is powerful.

Presumed competence is operating with the assumption that individuals have the ability to learn, communicate, and make decisions. When working with my students, I always want to presume competence. This mindset, along with moments like these, has shown me how Henry was aware of a lot more than we realized. As a result of this exchange of communication, when I came to his class and he heard my voice, Henry would get excited and bring his head up. When I sat next to him to talk to him, Henry started turning towards me. One time he laid his head on my shoulder.

The ability to understand as well as the realization that others can understand you when you communicate, is powerful.

When working with my students, I have to keep in mind my ultimate goal. It's about quality of life, which includes being able to understand one's world and interact with it. The ability to communicate is key. Communication is one of the most valuable tools I can give to my students. Communication involves being able to interact, understand, make choices, comment, and communicate one's thoughts as much as possible. A key part of communication involves literacy. So, we are helping Henry learn the alphabet. Right now the letter symbols are meaningless to him. But as we bring in the sounds of the letters and expose him to all the possibilities these letters and combinations of these letters bring, meaning will follow.

Understanding What One Is Looking At

The second puzzle piece necessary for vision to occur is the ability to understand what one is looking at. One of the aspects of CVI is that individuals may visually regard something but be unable to understand or process what is being presented to them. To be able to truly see something, one also needs to be able to identify what it is they are looking at. This takes time. When I want to show something new to my students, I need to figure out how to tie it into something they are already familiar with.

For example, one of my students initially was only able to see things that were blue. If I showed him a red comb, he would not be able to make out what it was. However, if I showed him a blue comb and combed his hair with it (a sensation he is used to), his understanding of what the blue comb is would increase, making his likelihood of taking in the comb visually and identifying it something he could palpably do.

There is always a certain level of vision that is present. My job is to find where that level is, what the child can see with comprehension, and then build on that to further understanding and development of vision. I strive to provide an understanding of the world around my students, thus enabling them to interact with it. We build on the familiar to bring understanding to the unfamiliar.

In the book of Acts, Chapter 17, Paul is in Athens, Greece. In this culture, there are many Greek gods that are worshiped. This is the first time this group of people is learning about Jesus. They don't have any understanding or previous experience with Jesus. Paul starts by talking about what is familiar to them. Something they can understand. He notices their statue to the "unknown god" and proceeds to introduce the reality of God through this statue. He used the knowledge they already possessed and built upon this so they could understand what he was trying to tell them (see Acts 17:23-31).

The Process of Understanding

Sometimes the ability to understand is a process. The book of Mark in the Bible tells of the time the disciples were in the boat with Jesus. They were talking amongst themselves about how they had forgotten to take bread with them. This was after witnessing Jesus performing the miracles of feeding thousands of people from just a little bit of food.

"They were discussing among themselves that they did not have any bread. Aware of this, he said to them, 'Why are you discussing the fact that you have no bread? Don't you understand or comprehend? Do you have hardened hearts? Do you have eyes and not see; do you have ears and not hear? And do you not remember? When I broke the five loaves for the five thousand, how many baskets full of leftovers did you collect?' 'Twelve,' they told him. 'When I broke the seven loaves for the four thousand, how many baskets full of pieces did you collect?' 'Seven,' they said. And he said to them, 'Don't you understand yet?'" (Mark 8:16-21 CSB)

In this same chapter, the disciples witness Jesus bringing sight to a blind man. In this case, it did not happen instantly. We may have an encounter with Jesus which opens our eyes. But it may take more encounters with Him to thoroughly grasp what He is showing us.

"They came to Bethsaida. They brought a blind man to him and begged him to touch him. He took the blind man by the hand and brought him out of the village. Spitting on his eyes and laying his hands on him, he asked him, 'Do you see anything?' He looked up and said, 'I see people—they look like trees walking.' Again Jesus placed his hands on the man's eyes. The man looked intently and his sight was restored and he saw everything clearly" (Mark 8:22-25 CSB).

The first time this man was touched by Jesus, his blindness was taken away, but he was not able to see and understand what he was looking at. He needed a second touch from Jesus to give him understanding.

With my students, reaching an understanding of a concept or idea is a process. Intervention has to be intentionally thought out and it takes time. It doesn't usually happen in one activity or lesson plan. This understanding comes through experiences and then keeping these experiences in our memory.

There is a reason God had His people build altars of remembrance, to remember the ways He had rescued them throughout history. Understanding comes with witnessing what God is doing along with remembering what He has done. The disciples found themselves in the middle of this process where they had experienced firsthand Jesus's miracles of provision but had not yet reached full understanding of who Jesus was. We may have an encounter with Jesus and have our eyes opened, but it may take more encounters with him to thoroughly grasp what He is saying to us.

We may have an encounter with Jesus and have our eyes opened, but it may take more encounters with him to thoroughly grasp what He is saying to us.

Understood Fully By God

"O Lord, you have examined my heart and know everything about me. You know when I sit down or stand up. You know my thoughts even when I'm far away. You see me when I travel and when I rest at home. You know everything I do. You know what I am going to say even before I say it, Lord. You go before me and follow me. You place your hand of blessing on my head. Such knowledge is too wonderful for me, too great for me to understand!" (Psalm 139:1-6 NLT)

This Psalm has brought me much peace as I have spent time allowing its truth to sink in. God is always up to date with what we are familiar with and how our individual brains work. It is amazing how God knows us better than we know ourselves. He understands why we think the way we do. He is even aware of what we're going to say before we say it! What we're going to write before we write it! I think of how I work with my students, each at their own level of functional vision. I take time to consider various methods and strategies to help them understand what they are seeing.

This is what God does for us. And while I do not fully understand how every brain functions with my students, God does. God understands exactly how our brain works and what we are able to process and what we are not. He knows where He wants to take us and how to get us there. When we genuinely believe this, supernatural peace floods our inner being that no circumstance or situation can take away.

And no matter how long the process is, God will continue working with us to gain understanding. Likewise, I will continue working with Henry and introducing letters. I won't give up because I believe that he can do it and I understand what the power of literacy can do for him. With time and that continued exposure, he will come to understand what each individual letter means and how they work together.

Seek, and You Shall Find

Are you going through something in your life that doesn't make sense where you don't understand what is happening? This could be experiencing a break in a relationship or a loved one struggling with health despite treatment, despite prayers. Finances that are a continuous struggle despite hard work and discipline. Dreams you once had that keep getting put on hold. I encourage you to bring these before the Lord. Remember that we never see the big picture, but we have someone who does.

Think back over your life and remember those times when God was faithful. Remember the tough situation where you didn't understand what was going on at the time, but how God came through. This is an important way to trust in God. Read through the stories in the Bible as another way to bolster your faith. The Bible is full of people who couldn't make sense of their life at some point.

In the book of Ruth, Naomi was questioning the death of her husband and her sons. She returned to her homeland bitter and empty. She had no idea of how she and Ruth would be provided for, no idea of the plan that God had in store for her and her family.

The story of Job is another story about a man who has lost everything —his children, wealth, health, friends. He lost it all and did not understand the reason at the time. What is amazing is how Job never lost his faith. He never broke communication with God but kept calling out to Him.

In both of these stories, God brought about restoration and more than doubled the amount of blessing. They demonstrate how God is for us, not against us. He wants to bring good to our lives. Like Job, continue calling out to the Lord for answers and guidance when you go through times like this. Jesus says, "Ask and it shall be given to you; seek and you will find; knock and the door will be opened to you" (Matthew 7:7 NIV).

I had to put in time and effort to familiarize myself with Henry and learn how to give him access to communication. It is still a learning process. But unlike Henry, we have access to a God who already sees with perfect understanding. And He wants to impart this to us. I believe it moves His heart when we faithfully search and seek to gain His understanding in all things. He honors this and is faithful. He knows each of us intimately, better than we even know ourselves. He grasps better than anyone how to bring us to an understanding of Him and His ways. Don't be shy. Ask God for whatever answers you are needing. He knows how to get through to you.

3

EXPERIENCES THAT PROVIDE MEANING

"I pray that the God of our Lord Jesus Christ, the glorious Father, would give you the Spirit of wisdom and revelation in the knowledge of him."
(Ephesians 1:17 CSB)

Two days before we moved my son Reilly into his college dorm his freshman year, something happened with my back where it started having spasms that were incredibly painful. Somehow I managed to be present the day we moved Reilly in. It was 2020, and due to Covid restrictions we would only be allowed to be in his dorm room this one day, and I wasn't going to miss out on that. His move-in date took place right after the Holiday Farm Fire where we had evacuated our home, all while starting the beginning of the new school year. My back locked up, and I could hardly move. It was my first time experiencing pain of this magnitude. The doctor gave me a shot and muscle relaxant along with heavy pain medication. I was referred for physical therapy the following week.

Fast forward to the fall of 2023 where I had another back spasm, and my back seized up on me again. Coincidentally, this was the day after I moved my daughter into her college dorm for her freshman year. My niece, Bree, is an amazing physical therapist. I had contacted her after what had happened to me during Reilly's move, and I reached out again. As I explained what was going on, she asked me if I could do a couple of movements, which I could. Bree had the training, expertise, and innate wisdom to determine that my back was perfectly healthy and strong. She surprised me by saying it made sense that my back reacted this same way as it did when Reilly moved out. Bree called it emotional muscle memory.

This type of muscle memory happens when emotions from previous events are stored at a cellular level in the body. These are often from traumatic experiences and can cause physical pain. The emotions need to be released for healing to happen. My muscles remembered the first transition of a child moving off to college along with all the events that took place at that time and reacted in the same way with my second child moving out. The intense emotions were expressing themselves in my body, and I had to retrain my brain to acknowledge that my back was fine and I was safe.

Bree gave me what I call "floppy exercises" to do that would help with the retraining of my brain. She gave me the ability to understand what was happening between my body and my emotions. With this understanding, I was able to overcome the pain and get full mobility within two days.

Being able to understand is a powerful thing. I have a sense that when Peter moves out to go to college, I will have a different experience because of what I learned from Bree.

Experiences Are What Provide Meaning

The third puzzle piece that needs to be present for vision to occur is meaningful experience. Once meaning occurs, memories are formed and stored in the brain. These memories are then brought up to the forefront every time something new is presented. They are used for cross-referencing to help identify the new thing. The more the visual library is built up with memories as a result of meaningful experiences, the more an individual can process what they are looking at and further understand the world around them.

Another example of providing experiences to bring about meaning and understanding involves my students who are blind. When I first started working as a Teacher for the Visually Impaired, our program would hold a two-week summer camp called the "Independent Living Skills Camp." The goal of this camp was to build understanding by focusing on basic skills that included common household tasks, grocery shopping, and cooking as well as other things. We also had leisure type activities such as horseback riding, canoeing, and swimming. One of our aims for this camp was to educate these students by helping them understand where things come from and provide meaning through first-hand experiences.

During this time, the students would each pick a meal to cook for the group. It is common for children who are blind to think that food magically appears in the kitchen and then on their plates. They have to be implicitly taught that one has to go to the grocery store to buy the food and bring it to the kitchen before starting to cook. By including them in the process, it increases their understanding, thus positively impacting their future independence and self sufficiency.

A favorite food the campers requested making for several years was pickles. For our students who were born blind, they knew pickles came in a jar. They had eaten them, but that was the extent of their experience with pickles. To provide this first-hand experience and understanding, we began with a visit to a farm. Our students learned that pickles are made from cucumbers, and this particular farm grew cucumbers. The campers then bought the cucumbers, cut them up, added garlic and spices, made the brine, and then put everything together in a jar. Pickles took on a whole new meaning after learning about and experiencing how they were made and what they were made from. Every time these students eat pickles now, they will be able to pull from their memory all they learned about pickles. This also provided the realization that most of what we eat has to go through a process before it lands on our plate.

Drawing Near

During the fall of 2019, I started attending conferences led by Soorin Backer. It was through these conferences that I first experienced the power of the Holy Spirit. I began to gain an understanding of how deeply loved and known I am by God. A whole new world opened up to me. At the first conference, I experienced a taste of what being close to God was like and wanted so much more. My hunger grew, and I began to get up early every morning to spend time reading my Bible and talking with God. It started with 20 minutes at a time, but then that wasn't enough. The closer I got to God, the more I desired Him. It wasn't how it used to be when I was younger and I was encouraged to have time dedicated every day to reading my Bible. Back then, it felt more like a chore. Something I had to do. I wasn't motivated, and it didn't hold the meaning it does for me now. That all changed when I understood the true meaning of what Christ did for me and the meaning of what life looked like living it alongside Him. Hope. Excitement. Adventure. Love. Healing. Joy. Peace. Faith against all odds. Now I am tenacious in my fight to have this time with God. I do everything I can to protect this time. It gives meaning to my life and sustains me.

What amazes me is my growing awareness of how God values this time with me even more than I do. One morning I was exceptionally tired and thought I could sleep a little longer. Then this image came into my mind of Jesus running and leaping in excitement going to "our place" to meet with me. I literally jumped out of bed in anticipation and excitement to be with Jesus. Song of Songs 2:8 (TPT) describes this well. "Listen! I hear my lover's voice. I know it's him coming to me—leaping with joy over mountains, skipping in love over the hills that separate us, to come to me."

The more we know God, the more we want to seek and draw near to Him. The result is a growing familiarity and personal relationship with God, not only learning about Him, but knowing Him. Actual experience. He wants to be known too. The true treasure is being in relationship with God, and the search along the way, is the experience.

Rewiring From Experience

We own an electric car that I use as an itinerant teacher driving around the school districts in our county. But it can only take me so far. My husband, Jon, drives an older car with a stick shift. Some days, I need to drive further than my electric car can go. We decided that, instead of buying another car, I would drive my husband's car on those days. It took me more than two years to conjure up the courage as I had had a couple of bad experiences involving a stick shift car long ago. With my daughter going away to college taking the other car with her, I knew I needed to get over this fear. To prepare myself, I practiced driving the car in a parking lot and then out on the road with Jon. The gears were a little finicky, but I could do it. It still took me a while before I worked up the courage to take it around from school to school for my job.

The day things changed was a Thursday when I realized I wouldn't be able to go to my Thursday group unless I drove the stick shift. It was finally time to make the choice to just drive the car. It took the whole day to conquer my fear that I would stall in the middle of an intersection or something worse. I kept telling myself I knew how to drive this car. Gradually, my mind came into sync with my heart telling me I could do this. By the end of the day, all fear had gone and I was confident in my driving skills. But it took a step of faith believing I could do it. I knew I could, but my mind was not yet aligned. My fear was steadily being stripped away as I drove, replacing my old negative experience with a positive one based on reality. And overcoming my fear saved us money from having to buy another car.

Choosing to Come Into Alignment

Replacing painful experiences with ones done in the reality of His truth can be life changing. What painful experiences from the past continue to tie you down? Are there experiences where irrational fear has a hold on you? Are there painful memories that need to be released from previous events? Do you have fear where your heart comprehends the truth, but your mind has not come into alignment with this truth yet? Do you struggle with physical pain, as I did with my back, where the root cause is emotional trauma?

When we become believers in Christ, our hearts are forever transformed. However, it is a lifelong process to bring our minds into alignment with our new identity in Christ. It is up to us to step out in faith and walk in this. This stepping out requires us to rewrite our experiences of the past that have left an imprint on our minds that is not from the Lord—an imprint that targets lies we have believed in, fears we have nurtured based on these lies. This is the part where God in His lovingkindness gives us the choice whether or not to pay attention to those imprints from the past. We can choose to step out in faith and allow Him to give us new experiences. Fresh imprints are then formed based on the reality of who we are in Him.

The choice is ours. The good news is we don't do this journey alone. He is with us every step of the way. He is always present and waiting for you to allow Him to transform your pain with new meaning based on His reality.

4

MOTIVATION AND TENACITY

"And consider the example that Jesus, the Anointed One, has set before us. Let his mindset become your motivation." (Philippians 2:5 TPT)

It was my last day in La Paz before flying back to Oregon. I had been on a trip to Bolivia with my parents and brother during April of 2019 to celebrate the 100-year anniversary of the Friend's Church. On this day my friend, Ana Maria, and I walked through the Max Paredes part of the city to the church we were visiting. Along the way, Ana said she wanted to stop and get some soup. She was hungry as she hadn't had a meal since breakfast and it was late afternoon.

We were about a block from the church when she pointed across the street to a restaurant sign. There was no door next to the sign, only a metal corrugated sheet that was pushed to the side revealing a small triangular-shaped room with benches along the walls and some stools. No one was inside yet, so Ana wanted to take advantage and get some soup before it got busy. The sign advertised: *sopa de cordero, sopa de res, sopa de pollo* (soup with sheep meat, soup with beef, and soup with chicken). A man tied a roll of toilet paper onto a wire hanging from the metal sheet, announcing that they were open for business. Next to the sidewalk along the busy road in front of the room, two women were readying three huge metal pots of soup. We crossed the street, went inside, and sat down on a bench. Others sauntered in after us, sitting down as well.

Steam poured out as the women lifted the lid off one of the pots. A man walked in to take orders. He asked whether anyone wanted *chuños* (freeze-dried potatoes) in their soup. At this point, an elderly man with a scowl on his face came in and sat across from us, and gave his order. The man taking orders started passing out bowls of soup. He handed one to a woman sitting a couple of seats to my right. She took the soup, stirred it around, and then declared she hadn't asked for *chuños*, and handed it back to the man. The man took the bowl and passed it to the old man. The man looked sternly at both the lady and the man who served the soup. He held the bowl for a few minutes without touching the soup and then tried to give it back. The serving man refused to take it, saying the soup was perfectly fine and that the woman hadn't even touched it. The old man declared that he wanted a fresh bowl and wasn't going to take soup that was given to somebody else. The tension in the room started to rise.

Meanwhile, Ana had received her soup, a large bowl with two potatoes and a huge meat bone with meat on it. Smelled good! She calmly ate (she is a slow eater!) while I wished she would hurry up so we could leave before the situation escalated more. The man taking orders continued his business, ignoring the old man. He came back between delivering soup carrying a bowl of *llajua* (spicy sauce made out of Bolivian chilies), offering it to each person. The old man tried to get his attention to no avail. Finally, he stood up and stomped outside, carrying the soup and placing it on the lid of one of the pots and stomped back inside and sat down. The ignoring continued.

Ana kept eating quietly, slurping up her soup. More people came until we were all sitting cheek to cheek—butt cheeks, that is. One lady asked for a *servieta* (a napkin). The man pointed to a small rope strung across the room holding two toilet paper rolls. Thanking him, she reached for some toilet paper. The man took some more orders, went out and got the bowl of rejected soup sitting by the pots of soup, and offered it to an unsuspecting newcomer, who gratefully ate it.

At this point, the scowl on the old man had deepened significantly, and he finally got up and went outside to confront the cook. He should have known better. The lady yelled at him for rejecting her soup and refused to give him another bowl. If her soup wasn't good enough for him, he didn't deserve any. They yelled back and forth for a while, and we all sat tensely, not quite sure what to expect. Somehow they came to an agreement, and the woman gave him a bowl of soup. The man came back inside, sat down, and finally began to eat. Ana finished soon after, and we went on our way.

It was four years later during the process of writing this book, that God revealed to me the meaning of my "soup experience". He showed me it was about the link between motivation and tenacity. That old man was highly motivated by his hunger, (not to mention his right to his own bowl of soup meant for him). That hunger in turn made him tenacious in his fight for the soup.

Hunger for God motivates me, and this hunger drives my tenacity to pursue a relationship with God. I believe He wants us to acknowledge the importance of each of us getting our own "soup". Soup that is specially made just for us. No one wants leftovers meant for someone else. This brings me back to how deeply God sees us. He sees us each individually and has a specific plan/thumbprint on our lives. At first, I had thought the old man represented something negative, but on reflection, I recognized his tenacity and unwillingness to give up and settle for something less. I saw his fight to persist to get something that was meant for him. Neither should we settle for something less.

I believe He wants us to acknowledge the importance of each of us getting our own "soup".

The Four Puzzle Pieces Necessary for Vision

Using the analogy of a four-piece puzzle, in order for the puzzle to be complete, these four pieces need to be in place. As we have seen in the previous chapters, the first piece is that the person needs to be attentive and alert. Second, they need to have the ability to understand what it is they are looking at. Third, in order to have this understanding, they need experiences that give meaning to this information. The last piece is motivation. In order to see, a person needs a reason to look towards something. I like to think of these four puzzle pieces fitting together to bring a complete picture. Each piece by itself is not enough. They all need to be present.

Vision requires significantly more energy in the brain to process than the other senses. When working with students with CVI, I have to schedule visual breaks as visual fatigue is a real thing. As stated earlier, vision can take up to 50% of the brain, whereas our other senses take a lot less energy. Depending on the student, for every five to ten minutes spent focusing on materials, I plan a one to two minute visual break.

The more the student understands what it is they are looking at, the more motivation arises to look for longer periods of time. Meaning needs to be attached to what they are focusing on for this to happen. One way of doing this is to tie the activity into an everyday routine, often with something that holds high interest for the student.

Currently, one of my teenage students, Victoria, is into Dolly Parton. Her team and I put together a themed unit about Dolly and pulled together activities that targeted the goals on Victoria's Individualized Education Plan (IEP). I made 3D books where, instead of pictures, actual objects from the story are provided. One of the books in the unit is Dolly Parton's book *The Coat of Many Colors*. In this book, I had each page feature a different single-colored cloth. The plan was for Victoria to take a piece of cloth from each page and place it on an outline of a coat she was putting together.

Within this activity, Victoria receives the opportunity to practice many skills including visual fixation. This visual fixation broadens from looking at a single-colored object to a multi-colored object, and to shifting her gaze from object to object. These skills help improve her ability to reach and grab the scraps of cloth, placing them on the coat outline. Victoria already loves this book and is familiar with the story. We have shown her the video of Dolly reading this story herself along with the song that goes with the book.

Using high-interest activities motivates my students. The tenacity of repetition plays a part in forming neural pathways and connections as meaning is reinforced.

The Importance of Tenacity

One of the definitions of tenacity is to grip something firmly and not let go. It means to persevere and persist without giving up. When I think of tenacity, Jacob comes to mind. The biblical Patriarch Jacob had tenacity from the get-go. I find it significant that this is recorded even from birth. In Genesis, we read about the birth of the twins and how Jacob came out of the birth canal holding onto Esau's heel. This tenacity shows throughout his life, although not always in the best light.

He and his mother were tenacious in obtaining the blessing and inheritance meant for his older brother, Esau. At this point this tenacity was motivated by greed. Deception and trickery were used to disguise Jacob impersonating as Esau when approaching his father, Isaac, who was blind in his old age. Isaac thought he was giving his blessing to his eldest son, but it was Jacob who received this blessing. Jacob and his mother's tenacity to get the blessing was done in such a way that relationships were broken and harm was done.

Jacob had to leave his parents and flee for his life. He had to pay a price for his actions, yet God still honored His promises to Jacob. He even encouraged him to not lose heart by speaking to him in a dream, telling him he would receive the blessing and inheritance promised through his father. The promise God gave Jacob in his dream displays God's tenacity and grip on Jacob's life. "The Lord was standing there beside him, saying 'I am the Lord, the God of your father Abraham and the God of Isaac. I will give you and your offspring the land on which you are lying. Your offspring will be like the dust of the earth, and you will spread out toward the west, the east, the north, and the south. All the people on earth will be blessed through you and your offspring. Look, I am with you and will watch over you wherever you go. I will bring you back to this land, for I will not leave you until I have done what I have promised you'" (Genesis 28:13-15 CSB). In time, this would change Jacob's motivation from greed to the desire that God's promises would be fulfilled.

One of the things I love about the story of Jacob is that God never let go of him. Even when Jacob acted selfishly and acted as a deceiver God didn't give up on him. But for Jacob to be ready to be used by God and receive the inheritance, his tenacity needed to be formed by motivation that was holy and pure. God worked on his character throughout the years he worked for his father-in-law, Laban.

Through all of Jacob's struggling and tenacity, one of the things he is most known for is when he struggled with God Himself. As Jacob left his father-in-law's land, before he was to cross over into the land promised to him, there came a night he was alone. During the night, a man appeared, and the two of them, Jacob and this stranger, engaged in a wrestling match. This struggle lasted through the night. In the morning, Jacob realized it had been God, who had taken on the form of the man with whom he had been wrestling, not letting go. This is when Jacob's name was changed to Israel because he had prevailed with God and man.

Even more than Jacob, there is another who is the greatest example of tenacity. Jesus. The Bible is full of verses that speak of His hold on us. His grip on our lives, never letting us go. His faithfulness displayed by His tenacity to the point of death on a cross, motivated by love. The ultimate sacrifice.

The Root of Our Motivation

We all have things that excite us, whether this be a hobby, a special interest, a job—activities or pursuits where when we aren't actively doing them at the moment, we can't wait to get back to them. The thing is, not everything that excites us is good. We can get swept up in the pursuit of wealth, knowledge, power, physical fitness, career advancement, even a relationship. Swept up to the detriment of our families and those who love us.

Whatever we are pursuing at the time may seem so right at the moment. How do we discern whether it is right or wrong? Whether it is from God or not? Is what you are doing being done in the sole interest of oneself, for selfish reasons? Or are your reasons fueled by love for God and those around you? Paul gives us guidance to discern these things.

Paul says: "Those who are motivated by the flesh only pursue what benefits themselves. But those who live by the impulses of the Holy Spirit are motivated to pursue spiritual realities" (Romans 8:5 TPT). Colossians 3:2 (NIV) tells us to "set our minds on things above, not on earthly things." The things of God are the spiritual realities Paul is referring to. It is for our benefit to focus on the things of God. His promises. His love for each of us. His grace that covers us. His faithfulness.

When you allow this new mindset to take over your life, you will discover that what formerly drove you will shift. You may still be driven, but your motive has changed. Jacob's motivation went from purely selfish reasons to becoming focused on others. Likewise, this inward transformation will impact those around you. Love for God transfers directly to love for others. Your motivation becomes outward in that "love and kindness are behind all you do" (I Corinthians 16:14 TPT).

Foreshadowing of My Life

My friend, Marie, gifted me a card with the word *tenacity* painted above a water lily on a lily pad. I researched the significance of a water lily and the lily pad itself. The lily flower stands for the resurrection of life. It closes itself at night only to reopen to receive the daylight the next morning. In other religions, the lily flower stands for enlightenment as a beautiful bloom emerges from the mud. I find it significant that water lilies help the environment as they rest on the water's surface. The flowers and pads provide shade keeping the water temperature cool protecting the fish and other living creatures underneath from the heat of the sun, like a thermostat. This temperature also prevents algae from growing in excess. Protection from predators, such as birds, serves as another important function of the water lily and lily pad.

When I think of the significance of the water lily and the lily pad as a metaphor for what God is calling me to do, something inside me comes alive. This is who I am and what I love to do. The extra bonus of lilies being aquatic plants ties into my love for water and is an extra gift from God, a hidden agate. It fits who I am. God showed me in His love how I am intricately seen and known by Him. This awareness motivates me and provides me with tenacity.

When I was a kid, in addition to gathering up sticks and stones, I would also line up all my stuffed animals and dolls to play school. I created my own curriculum, including reading books with the corresponding workbooks, math books, and spelling books. All made out of loads of construction paper stapled together. Little did I realize this playing was prophetic and would come to pass in time.

Many years later, during COVID-19, I dug into this deeper passion and started writing out different lesson plans for my current students. We were all working through Zoom. I did not want my students to fall through the cracks and was trying to think of effective teaching strategies in this new teaching era. What started as a few lesson plans grew to its own educational resource for students with CVI. There were a lot of challenges and hard work that went into writing this "curriculum", and at the time I had no idea of what it would grow to be. I only knew my students would benefit from it. My tenacity led me to finish what I had started due to love for my students. This new instructional resource is now being used in school districts throughout the United States and beyond.

I was motivated. My love for teaching combined with a desire to reach those students and families that could be forgotten provided the motivation to do what I did and the tenacity to stick with it.

Where Does Your Motivation Come From?

The old man with the soup was motivated by hunger. We aren't informed of his backstory or how hungry he was. Maybe he hadn't had a good meal in days. Regardless of the root of his behavior, he obviously was focused on his own needs at that moment. His thoughts were not about others around him. And there will be times when our thoughts need to be centered on ourselves. This may show up as a season of time when God wants you to focus solely on your relationship with Him. The outcome of that time will be an outpouring of His blessing on your life to others.

What season of life do you find yourself in? Is it a time when God wants to work on you drawing close to Him? Or is it a time when He is asking you to pour out to others?

What is amazing is that God has created us each with specific interests. These can be anything from riding motorcycles to traveling, from sewing to building houses. It could be sports, taking pictures, even being a tattoo artist. God is creative and loves diversity. When you follow God, you will discover that He will incorporate what you love to do into His plan for your life. He knows you so well and loves you so much that He desires you to have joy. He loves to have fun with you and to watch you have fun. I believe this is part of receiving "your own soup." Soup prepared specifically for you. So, pay attention to what you enjoy doing and hold onto it. God has a special soup waiting just for you.

5

GENERATIONAL BELIEFS
THE FIRST FILTER

"Do not conform to the pattern of this world, but be transformed by the renewing of your mind." (Romans 12:2 NIV)

I come from a strong heritage of God-loving ancestors. and I carry this with me in my own life. The family I was raised in was positive and warm, with parents who prioritized our spiritual growth. They also made sure to prioritize family time over ministry commitments, which I appreciate now, even if I didn't always as a teenager. Overall, I always felt loved and protected by my family.

However, in my extended family, a certain undercurrent seemed to flow, a pervasive sense of needing to strive in order to be accepted, to accomplish as many good works as possible. Being a missionary was considered the highest calling in the kingdom. Those of us who weren't called to be missionaries in the traditional sense may have felt belittled or overlooked. I bought into this lie and struggled with a lack of confidence that affected my day-to-day living.

Through digging deeper with my brother and talking with family members, I came to understand that these attitudes have been handed down through several generations. In my case, it resulted in assumptions of failure and never being good enough. Of being passed over and forgotten because I didn't fit into that missionary mold. Despite this "inheritance," I attribute where I am today and my own relationship with God as to how my parents raised me. I will be forever grateful for their wisdom and guidance.

I do want to mention that this erroneous belief system did not necessarily manifest in all of my extended family. It may have been something that I and a few others struggled with and were aware of. However, it is part of my story.

My grandpa always dreamed of being a missionary. His whole childhood was devoted to following this dream. When he married my grandma, they took off for Guatemala pregnant with my dad. During the first months in Guatemala, my grandma contracted cerebral malaria. Plans changed. Shortly after the birth, they had to move back stateside where Grandma lived the following years, periodically hospitalized from the mental effects of malaria. The Lord healed her ten years later, and she never had another recurrence.

Whenever my grandparents were in Oregon for our family reunions, Grandpa was always highlighting his sons, daughters, and grandchildren who were missionaries. I remember him approaching me and asking about the missionary work Jon and I were doing at the time, whether it was in South Korea, Saipan, or Ecuador. I clarified to him that we were public school teachers and not working in Christian schools or through a church organization. In those moments, I sensed his disappointment as the conversation always came to a halt. High praise appeared plentiful for others who were career missionaries with lots of prayer surrounding them, as there should be. But this should have extended to all regardless of vocation. Nevertheless, Grandpa gave me the best hugs, and I always knew I was loved by him.

Although my grandpa never entirely recovered from the disappointment of not being a career missionary, God did eventually give him and my grandma the opportunity in retirement to return to Guatemala for volunteer mission work.

Something shifted this last year for me as we had our annual Thanksgiving reunion. I wonder if I had been looking at this through the wrong filter. I felt this deep sense of belonging and acceptance that extended to all regardless of what anyone did for a living. The love that exists between the members of my extended family is deep. Vocation has nothing to do with the bonds that are present. As we sat in a circle joining our voices in song from the youngest to the oldest, tears formed in my eyes. I found I could not sing for the emotion deep inside that came up from being part of such an amazing family.

The truth is I have many relatives who lead amazing lives. Some may not fit the formal missionary definition, but each is a missionary in their own field. We have vet techs, teachers, psychologists, police officers, construction workers, entomologists, pastors, caretakers for the disabled, nurses, therapists, homemakers, artists, writers, musicians, actors, custodians and more in our family. An amazing legacy of equally valuable individuals.

The point is, for many years, this generational sense of not being good enough served as an inaccurate filter that prevented me from seeing a greater reality. And to be free, I needed these beliefs to instead be filtered through truth.

The Three Filters

Vision isn't a single sensory event but a multi-sensory experience. As an activity is experienced, this new experience has to go through a filtering process that attaches the new experience to existing memories. This gives the new information something to build on and expand, forming new neural pathways. Information that fails to attach to a memory is filtered out. This filtering process involves the thalamus.

The thalamus is a small organ in the middle of the brain behind the optic nerve. Although only two centimeters in size, it plays a huge role in acting as a filter for most of the sensory input from the outside world. The thalamus will only pay attention to a stimulus that makes sense or to whatever sensory modality is strongest at that time. If there is inadequate sensory information in one area, the thalamus may ignore this information and not pass it on to the cerebral cortex. For example, if an individual has strong auditory skills and weak visual skills, the thalamus is paying more attention to the auditory input and may disregard the visual input. As a result, the individual will have a harder time receiving visual information.

As I saw how the thalamus acts as a filter in the brain, I began to think about how we process all input we receive from those around us through our own filters. These filters either point us to truth or to an inaccurate picture of ourselves. As I thought about what these filters could be, I began to put them into three groups: generational, environmental, and experiences and memories. In this and the next two chapters, I will go into each of these filters and how we can apply the insights to our own lives. This current chapter deals with generational filters.

Generational and Family Beliefs

In the study of psychology, there is a term known as confirmation bias. Confirmation bias is the tendency we all have to seek out meaning and information that supports pre-existing beliefs. We place a higher value on information that supports these pre-existing beliefs, even if they may be inaccurate. One example of this relates to the students I work with. There is an assumption that if a student is nonverbal, they must be cognitively challenged. Those who hold this belief may conclude that when a child cannot answer back with a clear yes or no, it proves this point. This is confirmation bias. The confirmation bias passed down in my extended family seemed to be a belief that missionaries and pastors carried the highest heavenly calling, while the rest of us were not as important.

The way to break confirmation bias is to become aware of the beliefs you carry and begin questioning their validity. Be willing to be wrong. Search for ways to disprove the beliefs you have held onto that have no true foundation. When different situations arise, take time to listen to both sides of the story. Learn to view things from different perspectives. These are all good healthy measures to take to counter our natural tendency toward confirmation bias.

The phrase "The God of Abraham, Isaac, and Jacob" is found in the Bible numerous times. It demonstrates how beliefs carry over from generation to generation. There is something significantly spiritual in how beliefs are passed on through our bloodlines.

"I will establish My covenant as an everlasting covenant between me and you and your descendants after you for the generations to come, to be your God and the God of your descendants after you" (Genesis 17:7 NIV).

I recently learned about epigenetics from my cousin who is a psychologist. Epigenetics is the study of stable, heritable traits we have that have to do with our DNA. The content of our DNA does not change; however, the way it is expressed and its sequence can be impacted by the experiences of our parents, grandparents, and great-grandparents. Not everything in our DNA gets expressed and used. Some things are highlighted, while others are ignored, much like the sensory input coming into the thalamus. It has been believed for a long time that the DNA sequence that gets passed down from generation to generation cannot be changed. However, the study of epigenetics proves otherwise. The way we live our lives can alter the way our genes are expressed.

The way we live our lives can alter the way our genes are expressed.

I believe epigenetics can be tied to what we call generational curses. These are habits or behaviors that can be passed on from one generation to the next. They can include confirmation biases. Addictions, abuse, mental illnesses, physical illnesses, and even poverty can fall under generational curses. What gives tremendous hope in all this is the amazing truth that the studies of epigenetics demonstrate that we do not need to live under these curses! God's grace is greater than any sin or wrongful thinking that has been passed down through our family line.

When Moses met with God on Mount Sinai to be given the Ten Commandments, God gave this message: "The LORD, the LORD, the compassionate and gracious God, slow to anger, abounding in love and faithfulness, maintaining love to thousands, and forgiving wickedness, rebellion, and sin. Yet he does not leave the guilty unpunished; he punishes the children and their children for the sin of the parents to the third and fourth generation" (Exodus 34:6-7 NIV).

I have heard this passage being misinterpreted, creating fear that we are responsible for sin that has been committed by generations before us. But God does not hold us responsible for the sins that others have committed. In the book of Ezekiel, Chapter 18 describes personal responsibility for one's behavior and the outcome. If one follows God and does what is honorable and right, they will live. If one leads a life taking advantage of others and being dishonest, they will die. The chapter goes on to answer the question of what happens to a son who lives a righteous life but whose father committed numerous sins.

"As for his father, he will die for his own iniquity because he practiced fraud, robbed his brother, and did among his people what was not good. But you may ask, 'Why doesn't the son suffer punishment for the father's iniquity?' Since the son has done what is just and right, carefully observing all my statutes, he will certainly live" (Ezekiel 18:18-19 CSB).

Restoration

As noted previously, similar to the way the thalamus acts as a filter when vision first enters the brain, so we experience life through different kinds of filters. Which beliefs do you pay more attention to due to how you grew up? How have these beliefs influenced and shaped your life? Are they based on truth? Generational mindsets, along with family values, beliefs, the environment we grew up in, and subsequent experiences we have had all play a role in how we view life.

Beliefs are solid neural pathways that have been allowed to form in our brains. Neural pathways can be based on lies, on confirmation biases that have crept in. Beliefs that have been passed down through no fault of our own. If you have grown up within a family where a lot of lies were believed, establishing a false foundation, there is hope for transformation through God's truth.

The good news is that you are known by God. God is fully aware of your history and your family all the way back to Adam and Eve. Think back on your own family history. Spend some time and make a list of all the blessings and good things that have been passed down from generation to generation. Then go back and think about those things that aren't so good that have been present and negatively impacted your life.

Can you identify any unhealthy beliefs you have held onto that have been passed down? Maybe one gender was viewed as more important than the other, or children were meant to be seen and not heard. Maybe as a child, your acceptance was based on your performance versus your worth as a human being, a child of God. Maybe you were told by your parents when you were little that you could never do anything right or that you were always lazy. These are also examples of beliefs based on lies.

Regardless of what our family line looks like, we always have a choice to agree or disagree with untrue beliefs. When we agree with God's truth, the Bible shows His faithfulness towards us, His promises that He has only good in store for our future. Promises for freedom from addiction, deliverance from sin, financial provision, overcoming depression, freedom from fear and anxiety. God knows you and exactly what you need to be freed from. He knows how to restore truth to your life, truth about who you are in Him (see Jeremiah 29:11).

However, this can be an incredibly painful process. Facing our past takes tremendous courage. It often requires counseling and outside help. Through it all, know you are not facing this alone. I strongly encourage you to get the help you need.

Being aware of how what you believe impacts your own family can be life-changing for you and your family, for your own children and grandchildren. Recognize this as a wonderful opportunity to pass on what God has done for you. Demonstrating to your children their position in your family as your son or daughter can be a beautiful replica of the position we have with God our Father. Keep a record of how God has provided for your family and answered prayer. Read the story of those who have gone on before us in the Bible. Stories full of imperfect people who God used and was faithful to.

"Tell it to your children, and let your children tell it to their children, and their children to the next generation" (Joel 1:3 NIV).

Freedom. You do not have to live tied to your past. Hold onto the things that are good. Give to Him those attitudes, habits, behaviors, false beliefs that have been in your family line. Then sit back and watch Him work. Neural pathways can be rewired. Filters can be replaced. Harmful DNA sequences altered. Stories can be rewritten. It is never too late.

6

ENVIRONMENT
THE SECOND FILTER

"The name of the LORD is a fortified tower;
the righteous run to it and are safe." (Proverbs 18:10 NIV)

Picture this. You're a student placed into a loud and chaotic classroom. Posters of every size and type cover the walls, vying for space. Every single color possible swirling around, assaulting the senses. As you are in the room, anxiety builds up. You don't know what to look at, where to put your focus. Kids are all over the place. Some yelling. Some sitting looking bewildered. A classroom aide rushes by, chasing a boy while trying to block the doorway to prevent him from running down the hall. You are in the middle of it all, in a wheelchair, unable to duck or move to protect yourself if some object comes flying your way. You cannot make sense of what is going on around you and are unable to escape.

Unfortunately, many kids feel this way. The smallest detail out of alignment can send a child into a panic. This is especially true for students with CVI, where they are unable to understand and interpret their world. Other students around them may be having a hard time with their own behavior, adding to the mounting stress teachers and aides are experiencing, all affecting the environment.

When I step into a classroom experiencing this chaos, I ask the Lord what I can do. How can I help the situation, supporting both my students and the staff?

Last year I provided staff training on CVI to all teachers and aides who work in the LifeSkills classrooms in one of my districts. I explained how CVI can affect my students. The interventions and strategies I shared help all students but particularly those on my caseload. I was excited and hopeful to work together to incorporate these strategies and felt it important that I took the time to do this. But by the next year, most of the staff had left, and new people were in their place. I have done this training multiple times, just with individual teams. Education is a hard field to work in, and it is a constant push for most teachers to keep going. I struggled this last year wondering if I had it in me to start again. To retrain again. And again. And again.

There are classroom environments that are unsafe for my students with visual impairments. Classrooms where they are the ones unable to defend themselves if something unexpected happens. Many of my students are in wheelchairs, unable to even move themselves around. Unable to communicate. The visual stimulation makes it impossible to make sense of what is going on. The noise and movement, along with the tension in the room, makes them shut down. This situation may be due to no fault of the staff, but a combination of factors, including other students who have difficulty controlling their emotional behaviors and the challenge of managing this within the constraints of the law. The unfortunate reality is that my students in particular are the ones who keep falling through the cracks, seemingly forgotten in the chaos.

This isn't the case in all classrooms. There are classrooms I look forward to being in. Classrooms where if I am having a bad day, I appreciate that I can go visit to regain hope. Intentional structure is present, both physically in the classroom set up as well as in the organization of how they are run. The staff is consistent, which is vital to knowing the students and their individual needs enabling them to be proactive when challenging behaviors arise. These classrooms have high expectations for all, expectations of learning and bettering oneself. Expectations that one has the ability to communicate and be heard. It doesn't matter what form this takes, verbal or nonverbal. Real learning is happening, both life learning and academic. Students feel respected and safe. They are informed of what will happen next and what is required of them. They are willing to take risks in this environment and grow. Everyone is counted on to participate. It doesn't matter if one is nonverbal, in a wheelchair, or blind.

The emotional energy of an environment plays a role in creating an atmosphere that is either positive or negative, safe or threatening. I participated in a meeting a couple years ago. It was between the school team and a family who was not happy with the services being provided for their child. Contention and mistrust were conveyed in the tone of communication coming from the family towards the school. I recognized this family did not feel safe in the school environment. I remember praying in my spirit and asking God to work. This family was new to the district, and after listening to them talk about their past experience, I began to understand where they were coming from. How their past experience had given them the filter they were now looking through, assuming every school would treat their son the same.

The meeting was not going well, and we decided to resume the next day. During this break, I was able to talk with the school team and encourage them to approach this situation from a different angle. I encouraged the team to understand the fear the parents were facing with the possible loss of sight that was anticipated for their son. This was our chance to show this family that not all schools were the same. That we had the best intentions in serving their son and making sure his needs were met. This was our chance to show we cared.

By the end of this meeting, the school team's atmosphere had changed. Excitement had replaced frustration now in anticipation of meeting again with the parents, along with a challenge to show them they cared. A compassion that hadn't existed before was now present.

Hope. God was working and changing hearts. Changing atmospheres. Changing environments.

The Right Environment

When working with students with CVI, the environment plays a significant part in their ability to function visually. This is largely due to the unique characteristics that make up CVI. Half of the approach in working with a child with this diagnosis is understanding how to create the right environment for that child that meets their level of functional vision.

Matt Tietjen, a Teacher for the Visually Impaired, has put together a way to measure the environment a student is placed in. This method helps determine whether or not it is an environment in which the student can be successful in. Matt checks out the amount of visual information in a room, how loud the room is, how much movement is present, and the type of lighting. Matt observes familiarity versus unfamiliarity of the location. The degree to which these elements are manifested play a part in creating an environment that can feel either safe or threatening. If a student experiences anxiety, they will not be successful learners. It is crucial to know your student and set up their environment in a way that will set them up for success where they feel safe enough to focus on learning.

God Is Our Refuge, Our Hiding Place

I had a vivid dream last year where my friend, Marie, and I were driving in the countryside looking for the perfect picnic spot. We kept passing these beautiful areas, but God was telling us to keep driving. It wasn't until the end of the road we were shown our place, a beautiful meadow on the edge of a large pond. The pond had lily pads all over it, and there was a large oak tree that provided shade over the meadow. We couldn't wait to spread a blanket and lie out on that meadow with our picnic. The presence of joy, hope, and laughter saturated us as we spent time together in His presence. That image has become one of my safe places with the Lord.

Safety is a basic need we all share in order to live a healthy and productive life. It allows us to let down our guard and be who we are meant to be. It allows us to take risks so we can learn and grow, helps us make and maintain friendships where we can open up freely and be ourselves.

I have struggled with this issue for much of my life. I am fortunate that the one consistent place I felt safe was home with my family. But outside my home, I struggled with not feeling safe. Not feeling safe with people, whether this was in school, church, or other places. I am blessed to have friendships where I have the freedom and security to be who I am. I think of my childhood friend, Anita, with whom I can share anything and be unreservedly myself. She understands and accepts me. Safety. I think of my Thursday group of women who I can come to with anything. In this group, I am free to be who God has called me to be and exercise the gifts He has given me. I am safe and secure and can let my loud and goofy side show. Safety. I have other friends who I may not be loud and goofy with, but with whom I am comfortable and secure talking about spiritual things and what is going on in my life. Safety.

There are different aspects of safety we may experience with different people. There are friendships where we feel safe showing certain parts of ourselves but keep other parts hidden. I have wondered if there exists a relationship on earth where we can fully be ourselves and feel accepted. People are imperfect and will always let us down at some point. That's where God comes in. I'm reminded again of Psalm 139 and how God is completely familiar with all our ways, past, present and future as well as with who we are as individual people. He knows how we will react in certain situations, and with this He comes behind us protecting us from our past, and goes before preparing the way. His thoughts on us number more than the grains of sand on earth. We have complete safety in Him, (see Psalm 139).

Because of the fall of man, the world is not a safe place. Evil exists and enemies are lurking around every corner. Paul tells us that "our struggle is not against flesh and blood, but against the rulers, against the authorities, against the powers of this dark world and against the spiritual forces of evil in the heavenly realms" (Ephesians 6:12 NIV).

How do we find safety in the midst of this? Similar to how I try to create a safe environment for my students, God has a place for us where we are safe. The difference is that for my students it may not be possible to have a consistently secure environment, but our safe place with God is always available (see Psalm 91).

One of my favorite passages is Psalm 18. I love the Passion translation of the second verse.

"Yahweh, you're the bedrock beneath my feet, my faith-fortress, my wonderful deliverer, my God, my rock of rescue where none can reach me. You're the shield around me, the mighty power that saves me, and my high place" (Psalm 18:2 TPT).

Other translations say that God is our rock. Bedrock is the solid rock beneath all other soil and earthly materials. Bedrock also means the principles or ideas on which something is based. God is my bedrock. He is my fortress. A fortress is a building or structure that is built so enemies have difficulty entering. God delivers me and rescues me, bringing me to a high place where none can reach me. Complete safety in Him. His presence is with me throughout the day. Because of Him, I can create or bring my environment with me wherever I go. This safety, 24/7, is available to all who believe in Him. It's our choice to live in it.

Becoming a Safe Place

What was your family environment when you were a child? Was it a safe place where you were able to grow into the person God created you to be? Or did you grow up in a home where your parents or caretakers placed value on your performance and what you accomplished over who you were as a person? Was the love and acceptance conditional? Or were you valued simply because you existed? I have often observed that unless we face and resolve these questions, we tend to bring the environment we grew up in into our present surroundings.

One of the most heartbreaking things for me is watching children, teenagers, and adults live in constant tension not knowing if home is a safe place because acceptance is based on following the rules. Sadly, this is transferred to how we view God. Do we view God as someone we have to please? As someone we have to earn our way to being accepted, where our value is conditional? Where God acts more as an employer who can fire us at any moment based on our actions? Or are we able to live in the security that we are accepted as we are just because we are His son or daughter? These can be incredibly painful and hard questions to face.

As God's children, we have full access to Him. As His children, we are heirs with full rights passed down to us. All because He loves us. I was deeply impacted by a sermon I once heard where the pastor used the metaphor of how each of us are given house keys the moment we believe in Jesus. Keys that will never be taken away. Keys that signify our belonging and being part of the family of God. All that is asked of us is to believe in who God says He is and receive. "Yet to all who did receive him, to those who believed in his name, he gave the right to become children of God" (John 1:12 NIV).

Maybe the unsafe environment for you was outside your family home due to being bullied as a young child and made fun of. Maybe you are in an abusive relationship or in a work environment with a threatening boss. Maybe you have friends who have been wrongfully accusing you. All situations that make us feel unsafe.

Our God is a God of hope. Hope, the expectation that things will get better.

Our God is the God of the impossible! He sees you and understands everything about you. He is totally aware of the household you grew up in. Whether or not you grew up in an environment that provided security or find yourself in an insecure situation right now, He wants to bring the security of His love and acceptance to you. But do you know this? He loves you so much that He died for you. If you were the only person in the world, He would still have gone through dying on the cross for you without a moment's hesitation. That is how much He loves you. This love is unconditional. You cannot earn it, and you cannot lose it. It is secure.

The thing is... until you have experienced this love for yourself, change probably won't happen, but when you come across God's love in a personal way and allow Him to come into your heart, the impossible becomes possible. The more you encounter God's love and spend time with Him, the more you realize how thoroughly seen and known by Him you are, the more hope for change grows. To run into a love like this and be accepted, is incredible, awesome, life-changing! It brings immeasurable hope! And as He does this, you are more and more able to extend this safety of love, hope, and acceptance to others. Through Him, we have the ability to influence whatever circumstances we find ourselves in to usher in His presence. His presence brings peace, joy, love, kindness, gentleness, hope, goodness, self-control. We have the ability to be atmosphere changers wherever we go!

The more you encounter God's love and spend time with Him, the more you realize how thoroughly seen and known by Him you are.

It's like setting up a classroom where, because students feel safe, they can focus on learning and growing, even take risks. Is your home a setting where risks can be taken? Where growth and learning are occurring? A place where your children look forward to coming back to? What about where you work? The friendships you carry? Do others feel safe in your presence? Being open to God allows this to happen. For me, it is about loving Him and wanting to give Him my all. Giving up control of my life to Him so He can work through me to change the atmospheres around me to touch others, leading to changed environments. It's a bit of an oxymoron as releasing control to God is a scary step to take, but it leads to the most secure and safe place we can be.

7

EXPERIENCES AND MEMORIES
THIRD FILTER

"Now may the God of peace himself sanctify you completely. And may your whole spirit, soul, and body be kept sound and blameless at the coming of our Lord Jesus Christ." (I Thessalonians 5:23 CSB)

Growing up, I was part of a faith community that did not practice water baptism. My husband Jon and I attended several churches of other denominations while living overseas where water baptism was practiced. Yet I never had the urge to get baptized this way because I had always viewed baptism through the filter of Quaker beliefs. In my head, I saw the laying on of hands when I committed my life to the Lord as the baptism of the Holy Spirit. It was a meaningful experience back when I was a junior in high school. For me to get baptized by water meant that previous baptism of the Holy Spirit had no meaning for me, which wasn't true.

Looking back, if I was honest, it became more of a pride issue to not be baptized with water. As God was working in my life in my later 40s, I felt this nudge to be obedient and follow through with baptism. It held great meaning for me in that it was about me dying to my old self and identifying with Jesus dying on the cross for me, then rising again in the new life with Christ in me. It was a physical representation of what was taking place inside my heart, incorporating muscle memory with what was happening spiritually. As the physical and spiritual/mental/emotional aspects of myself were all being touched simultaneously, new neural pathways were forming.

As I was practicing pin-point obedience when I felt God nudge me, along with new understanding on the meaning of water baptism, I made the decision to follow through and be baptized. It was an incredible experience for me as my good friend and pastor baptized me. What is even more incredible is a friend in the audience took two pictures of my pastor hugging me after being baptized, another hidden agate. The hugs were exactly how I picture Jesus hugging me when I read Song of Songs, "His left hand cradles my head while his right hand holds me close. I am at rest in this love" (Song of Songs 2:6 TPT). It was another whole-body experience with more neural pathways formed as I experienced myself totally loved.

Whole Body Experiences

We are created in the image of God. Our brains are created the way they function on purpose. God intended us to have whole-body experiences to learn about and be in relationship with Him. These whole-body experiences act as filters to clarify and purify our understanding by removing wrong information. It is similar to going over past experiences and reliving them through God's truth.

As a Teacher for the Visually Impaired, one of my goals when working with students with CVI is to find ways to make sure visual information is getting past the thalamus to the visual cortex. Once this happens, I move on to bring in the rest of the sensory modalities (hearing, touch, taste, smell) to work simultaneously with vision. Vision does not occur on its own but is part of a multi-sensory process. Vision and the ability to process what one is looking at occurs when all sensory input is being cross-referenced and taken into account. When I work with a student, I address vision first because it is the sense that takes the most energy for the brain to process. As vision occurs, I start to bring in the other senses for meaning to come in.

When explaining how this works and to demonstrate the importance of "whole-body/sensory-rich" experiences, I like to use the example of a basketball. When we think of a basketball, we not only picture its appearance but also what it feels like, what it sounds like when bounced, and even what it smells like. Our brain naturally involves our other senses to bring meaning to what a basketball is. As this happens, we are building neural pathways regarding the concept of a basketball. This information is stored as a memory that we can later reference when we come across a similar object. These memories build connections where more neural pathways are then formed.

When working with a student, this concept of a whole-body experience may resemble something like this:

I start with vision first when the child is most alert and has the most energy to engage. A basketball is presented against a black background with a flashlight shining on the ball. This gives the child the support they need to be able to see the ball. Once they catch sight of the basketball, you know the visual information has passed from the thalamus onto the visual cortex. After the visual part has been addressed, I provide the opportunity to explore the ball with their hands. Most likely they will not be looking at the ball during this time as the thalamus is taking in the tactile input. I then tap into the auditory sense and bounce the ball so the child can discern what it sounds like. Repeating this sequence will strengthen this new neural pathway and the child will begin to learn what a basketball is. It may take many exposures of this same activity for the child to process, but those neural pathways are being solidified. This is where tenacity comes into play. When I sense the child is ready, I start combining the sensory modalities. I may even observe the child do this on their own. For example, if they are used to the tactile sensations, they may start looking at the ball while simultaneously holding it.

Exposing a student with CVI to this type of sensory-rich experience is a creative and versatile process. Using our basketball example, one can talk about the concept of the ball being round and being orange. We can then show an orange (the fruit) to a student and tie in those two characteristics. Now we have a chance to talk about size, squishiness, texture, smell of an orange. We can peel the orange and get a stronger smell, then go into taste. We can bring in the concept of peel and then introduce a banana. There are virtually unlimited options to continue building neural pathways. And all of these pathways result in memories the student will use to connect more confidently to their world around them.

Whole Body/Spirit Experiences

God uses whole-body experiences incorporating our senses to help us know Him and minister in meaningful ways to others. He uses these experiences to filter out the lies we've believed that have affected our life.

God uses whole-body experiences incorporating our senses to help us know Him.

Two years ago during Christmas, a couple of my close friends were going through some tough seasons in their lives. I spent time praying for them and asking the Holy Spirit if there was anything I could do to encourage them. The idea came to me when working on a project for one of my students with CVI. I incorporated my three main tools: making use of color, light, and movement. These tools help with that first attention piece that needs to be present for vision to occur to lead into a whole-body experience.

My intention was for my friends to see that God was working behind the scenes for them. I wanted them to look at their individual situations through the filter of God's perspective. I started to create a physical experience full of meaning that would counteract how it can feel when you are in the thick of a problem and God may seem absent or distant. I went searching for the perfect bottles to buy. With agates collected throughout the years, I applied these on the outside surface of the bottles and placed slow twinkling lights inside. This produced the physical representation of color, light, and movement I was aiming for. I shared how these agates represent the broken parts of our lives. When we give these parts to God and allow His light to shine through, beauty comes forth. I encouraged my friends when times were hard to turn off the room lights, leaving only the lights in the bottle on. Light always shines the brightest in the dark. The movement of the lights remind us the Holy Spirit is always working behind the scenes, even when we may not be aware of Him.

Whole-body experiences can also be applied to the spiritual practice of prayer. Praying can look differently to people. Thinking about how we are created and how our brains work, I am learning more and more how whole-body experiences influence prayer. I have always wondered how those who can just sit and pray for others are able to do that for long periods of time. I try to do that and my mind constantly wanders. Then comes the guilt struggle.

It wasn't until a couple of years ago that I learned my own personal prayer language. For me, it's through playing the piano. It correlates with that whole-body experience. My fingers move as I take in the music, and my mind is free to get lost in the sound. It empties out all those wandering thoughts, and people come to mind as I play. Melodies of songs impress themselves on me for certain people, and I am able to lift them up to God and allow the Holy Spirit to pray through my fingers to their specific needs. Sometimes I get a glimpse of these needs, sometimes not. When I feel led to share with people how I played for them, it is very encouraging and exactly what was needed in that moment. I am always in awe of how God works. This is another way that shows He knows me and speaks to me in a way I will understand.

Bringing the Physical and Spiritual Together

The definition of sanctification is the action of making something holy. It is the process of being purified, becoming pure. I love how Paul talks about sanctification happening through our whole spirit, soul, and body. You cannot separate these three aspects. We are all in the process of being sanctified to become sound and blameless. Being sound means to have a faith that is grounded in Christ and His truth, a firm foundation. Being blameless means you cannot be accused of wrongdoing. You are willing to be taught, to be led to do what is right in all situations. This process of sanctification goes hand in hand with whole-body experiences as we are being transformed more into His likeness each day.

Where do you find yourself in this process? What past experiences do you have that continue to produce fear or pain? Are you able to go back and view these experiences through God's truth? Are you willing to be led by Jesus, realizing He is right beside you as you do this? How can you incorporate a whole-body experience that will bring healing to your spirit, soul, and body? Experiences that will alter your perceptions of how you see the past and instead provide you a pure filter of God's love for you and the abundant life He has for you?

How does God speak to you? Think about all your senses, not only your auditory sense. You may have the ability to "hear" God more through visual means, tactile means, even means involving your sense of taste and smell. There are additional senses besides these five main senses that involve spatial awareness, and balance; our kinesthetic and proprioceptive senses. What is your unique language with Him?

I have a friend who paints and talks with God through her painting. Another friend who communes with God through her running and dancing. A friend who smells the fragrance of God in various places. My brother has discovered flagging and will pray for hours through flagging. I have friends who are very aware of both the presence of God and angels in a room. All are whole-body experiences that tie in multiple senses. None are better than another, but all valid and special in their uniqueness. All of these whole-body experiences can help in healing and bringing about wholeness, giving a correct perception of God's reality. Along with this comes the joy of discovering Him, knowing Him, and realizing you are known by Him.

God commanded His people in the Old Testament to build altars commemorating encounters with Him. These altars were a physical remembrance of Him working in the lives of His people, during those specific times neural pathways were being changed. God continues to encourage us to not forget what He has done in our lives. In order to keep these new pathways fresh and from reverting back to the old ways of thinking, a physical representation of what God has done is a way to solidify that muscle memory into the brain. It's bringing the whole-body experience to a culmination, bringing it all together.

Our altars will be different from each other's as God speaks to us individually. It can be as simple as printing the pictures I have of my friend hugging me after my baptism, or it can be as complex as writing a book. What do your altars look like? Do they convey the message of how well God knows you?

PART II

VISUAL CHARACTERISTICS

8

THE NEED FOR LIGHT

"Your lives light up the world. For how can you hide a city that stands on a hilltop? And who would light a lamp and then hide it in an obscure place? Instead, it's placed where everyone in the house can benefit from its light. So don't hide your light! Let it shine brightly before others, so that your commendable works will shine as light upon them, and then they will give their praise to your Father in heaven." (Matthew 5:14-16 TPT)

In the last couple of years, the power of our names has repeatedly been brought to my attention. At a back-to-school training for work, one of the themes was our identity. We were given an exercise where we had to think about our names and if we identified with them. Did they fit who we were as individuals? After we answered this question to ourselves we were encouraged to share with our group.

A year before this, I had attended a conference led by Soorin Backer. One of the sessions had to do with the power of our names. I already knew what my first name meant. Kristin: a follower of Christ. But I never knew what my second name meant. Elaine: a bright shining light. I remember being shocked when I learned this. It totally went against all those lies I believed about myself. It was one of those life-changing moments when I could sense my neural pathways begin to change. Something resonated deeply within me with this new revelation into who I was.

Up to this point, I had never been forthright about my faith. Teaching in the public school system, we are not to share our faith unless asked, which almost never comes up. So, it was something I kept to myself. I also had this fear within me that I would not be accepted if I shared this part of me. I had a decision to make. Would I stop hiding and share my name and its meaning? Or would I continue my old habit of cowering and bowing out? I knew in that instant that I wanted to follow God and start living into the identity He was calling me into.

When it came to my turn, I shared my name, "Kristin Elaine", and what it meant. I was a follower of Christ and a bright shining light. I declared that I did indeed identify with my name! To my surprise, I was accepted, and we moved on to the next person. It was like my colleagues already knew this about me. Relief and new courage surrounded me.

The Need for Light

Individuals with cortical visual impairment have certain characteristics unique to this diagnosis. These characteristics include visual needs, certain preferences, difficulties to overcome, and connections to be made. For the purpose of this book, I will refer to the ten CVI Characteristics defined by Dr. Roman-Lantzy in her assessment called the CVI Range Assessment. The following chapters in Part 2 will cover each of these characteristics.

One of the first characteristics is the need for light. Light plays the important function of illuminating and revealing what is being presented. It directs the child where to put their visual attention. Light can be used to both direct the eyes towards something in particular that is lit up, or to highlight a separate object. Highlighting can be done either by shining light on that object or providing backlighting. The use of light depends on a lot of factors, including what Phase an individual is in.

Out of the three phases of CVI taken from Dr. Roman's CVI Range Assessment, a child who is in Phase I of CVI may display the behavior of light gazing, where they cannot look away from a light source, whether this be a window, a light in a room, or the sun. As a child progresses beyond Phase I exhibiting more visual behaviors, light gazing will decrease and they will start being able to look away from the light. They still benefit from the support of a light shining on a presented object or being backlit by light, such as using a lightbox or screen.

When I work with my students, I have to be mindful about how I am using light. Depending on their needs, I may be presenting materials in front of a lightbox to help draw their attention. Maybe they have moved past this and what I do is shine a flashlight on an object being presented to them. What is important is that at this point they are not distracted by the light, but are looking at what the light is highlighting.

How Light Affects Our Past

Light shines the brightest in the dark. During the day, the furthest we can see is around 62 miles away. This is the edge of the Earth's atmosphere and space. Look in the same direction at night and you can see so much further. With the naked eye on a moonless night, one can see the Andromeda Galaxy, a collection of stars that is around 2.5 million light years away!

A child in Phase I may need a dark environment in which to present a lighted object to elicit visual attention. Those dark seasons in our lives may be what is needed to draw our attention to where it needs to be. I don't believe that God causes dark seasons in our lives. Those often come from our own choices or situations out of our control. He does, however, use these times in our life to draw us near to Him if we allow Him to.

**Those dark seasons in our lives may be what is needed
to draw our attention to where it needs to be.**

It's interesting how when we are going through those dark seasons of
our lives, daily distractions tend to take a less prominent place in our
attention. Those things that are truly important are highlighted. It's
like our vision is more focused during these times and we can see
more clearly.

One of the darkest times of my life was when Jon and I learned about
both our boys and their diagnosis, with first being told that Peter was
blind. Certain things that used to matter to me no longer held the
same importance. Whether this was keeping up with the news at that
time, being involved in certain social groups, shopping for clothes,
etc. All things good in their own right, but not needed for survival. It
was like I honed in and had laser focus on my own kids, especially
Peter, at that time. All the developmental milestones, no matter how
small for typical babies, were huge hurdles for us and meant to be
celebrated. In time, I was able to open up my "visual field" to let in
more of life around me again. To appreciate and enjoy things I
used to.

Light can also bring redemption to our past, no matter what we have
done or what has been done to us. God is aware. Psalm 139:5 talks
about how God follows behind us to spare us from the harm of our
past. As we come to Him, he redeems our past. Isaiah 61:7 NIV says
"Instead of your shame you will receive a double portion, and instead
of disgrace you will rejoice in your inheritance. And so you will
inherit a double portion in your land, and everlasting joy will be
yours." Jesus shares a parable in Matthew 20 about a landowner
hiring workers during different times of the day. Regardless of when
they started working, each person got paid for a full day. Even those
who came at the last moment and worked the last hour (see Matthew
20:1-16).

My grandparents on my mom's side discovered faith in Christ in their
later years. My granddad made the decision to follow God less than
one year before he died. I believe that last year was full of a double

portion of God's blessing of peace as he walked in his newfound faith. During his last year, my granddad was in so much pain from sickness that the doctor said he could have morphine whenever he wanted. Yet, throughout this time, he told my mom he had never been so at peace before. It is never too late to come to God.

Most of the time, when we are in the middle of a dark period of our life, we cannot envision the way out. However, when we can think back to that time a month later, a year later, we are amazed at how God carried us through. At how faithful He was providing for our every need at that critical time, protecting us as he kept us from the harm of our past, then present situation.

How Light Affects Our Present

The power of light! It causes darkness to flee. Light is an actual substance that affects the atmosphere. It dispels hopelessness and despair. It brings clarity. It reveals what is otherwise hidden. It illuminates every situation bringing a fresh perspective.

As light dispels darkness, it brings with it hope. One of the most meaningful parts of my job is when I go to a home to do the initial visual assessment of a child as part of the referral process to begin services. Often the family is in the grieving process as they have recently received the diagnosis. Prior to this visit, I go over the medical records and what the doctors have said concerning the visual implications from this diagnosis. When I start the evaluation, the first thing I do is ask the parents to tell me about their son or daughter.

When CVI is confirmed on the report, parents tell me how they've been told their child cannot see and is blind. Often tears are involved as they retell what the doctor said. Due to CVI being a relatively newer diagnosis, many doctors are not trained in how to work with someone who has this condition. They do not understand how to elicit visual behaviors, and so the child may very well come across as blind. This is when I can offer hope and a fresh perspective. There is always some level of vision present. My job during this first evaluation is to find out where this visual behavior exists and bring it out. It is a highpoint when this visual behavior is displayed and active looking is taking place. In the background, the parent is coming to the realization that their child is not totally blind after all. Strategies and tools are available to enable this existing vision to be used functionally. Guidance will be given on how to use these tools, and depending on the diagnosis, visual development can be expected to improve with this intervention. Hope. A fresh perspective.

How Light Affects Our Future

Light can also act as a guide for our future. There are many verses in the Bible that talk about God's Word being a light to our path (see Psalm 18:28, 119:105). I think of the role a sighted guide plays for a person who is blind. They walk slightly ahead with the person who is blind grasping their arm right above the elbow. This allows the person who is blind to perceive any slight turn and/or step up or down and walk accordingly. They are able to travel safely this way and can anticipate what is ahead through the movements of the sighted guide. In a similar way, the Holy Spirit guides us when we involve Him in our lives. As He follows behind us to spare us from our past, He also goes ahead into our future to prepare the way (see Psalm 139:5).

I have experienced His guiding me in several ways, including having specific verses stand out to me at different times in my life. I have had dreams where God speaks to me directly, and prophetic words have been spoken to me through others. One of the ways I have learned to pray is to ask God to either open or close doors. Often God only shows me the next step, and it's up to me to walk in obedience, realizing that after I take that step, He will then show me the next.

During the early years of our marriage, Jon and I had just come back to Oregon after teaching in Saipan for two years. We wanted to continue to teach overseas but did not have a job at this point. Money was tight, but by faith, we flew to Philadelphia and attended an international job fair for teachers. Through this job fair, we received requests from three different schools. We went to bed that night and asked God to close the doors to the countries He did not want us to go to. The next day He closed each door. We ended up leaving the job fair with nothing and most of our money spent. However, we clung to the knowledge that God knew what He was doing and was guiding us.

A week later while Jon was away counseling at a boys camp, I received a phone call from a school in Ecuador. We ended up being hired to teach at the American School of Guayaquil. While this teaching job did not turn out to be a long-term placement, it allowed us to spend two vacation months in Bolivia where I introduced Jon to my childhood home, friends, and family. God knew how important this was to me and how it was not something we could have done otherwise.

Before the time of Jesus, God's people, the Israelites, were living in a time of much turmoil. They were living under the Roman empire, and persecution and suffering were prevalent. Throughout this time, God spoke to His people through His prophets telling them deliverance was coming so as to encourage them to not lose hope. This deliverance would come in the form of a baby born and placed in a manger, who would be the Messiah, the One who would rescue His people from sin. These prophecies are strewn throughout the Old Testament, at least 300 of them, that point to Jesus's birth, death, and resurrection. Every one of these were fulfilled.

God still works through the prophetic voice. Often God gives us glimpses into what He has planned for us by speaking through others, shining light into our future. I have been given prophetic words throughout the past few years from people who knew me well as well as from others who were unfamiliar with me. These words have been greatly encouraging and given me something to hold onto whenever I start to doubt myself. Looking back now I can recognize how things have fallen into place and correlated with what I was told at that time. God does indeed go into our future to prepare the way.

Some of these words given to me included being told that I am someone who loves to watch lightning storms, specifically in relation to neural pathways being formed in the brain. I was told I love to go on scavenger hunts when I am learning and searching for answers to figure out how things tie together. These words immediately got my attention because they are true. What's amazing is these were said by people who were not familiar with me at the time. Unknown to them, I was in the process of putting together my VistaQuest BaseKit for children with CVI.

I remember being with my Thursday group a year earlier where we were praying for one another. My two friends, Betsy and Marie, prayed over me and it felt like a corkscrew was going into my brain (without pain). The following week was Spring Break, and God brought so much clarity in the direction of my BaseKit. I ended up writing much of the manual during that time. Like the verse in Ephesians 1:18 from The Passion Translation, God's light literally illuminated my imagination and flooded me with revelation in what I was to do. He prepared the way ahead for me.

How Is His Light Shining in Your Life?

Does the way you live your life point others to Jesus? Or do you find yourself hiding your light? The fear of man is often the barrier to letting your light shine. A fear of what others may think. I know this firsthand as it has been a struggle of mine for most of my life. Getting to a place where your relationship with God becomes more important than the approval or disapproval of others is where your life begins to change. You become more focused on the things of God than the things of this world. Your life becomes a shining light on a hill. A beacon of hope (see Song of Songs 7:14, TPT).

As God enables us to shine and let our light touch others, He also shines His light into our lives. I encourage you to take some time and think about your life from God's perspective. Go back to those times in your past, predominantly periods of your life where you sensed a lot of darkness. This may be a difficult childhood, an abusive marriage, a break in a relationship, the loss of a loved one, a time when finances were a struggle. Allow God's light to shine on these times to give you an understanding of how He was present and working behind the scenes. How did your character emerge from these dark times? Did you allow God to work? If there are remaining unresolved issues, will you allow God to work through those now in order to redeem what was lost?

Now take some time to bring a present situation before the Lord where you need a fresh perspective. Things may appear hopeless, but we serve a God of hope. God sees the whole picture whereas we are privy only to a part.

Are you at a crossroads with some weighty decisions to make concerning your future? God has already gone into your future to prepare the way. When your faith needs bolstering, remember how God showed his faithfulness in the past. In the same way, he is preparing you now for what lies ahead. He always comes through.

9

THE NEED FOR MOVEMENT

"If anyone is thirsty, let him come to me and drink. The one who believes in me, as the Scripture has said, will have streams of living water flow from deep within." (John 7:37-38 CSB)

I have always been drawn to water. As a young child I learned to swim in the hot springs of Urmiri in Bolivia. I had a short career being on the swim team at the high school in La Paz before moving to Oregon. Between vacation trips to Peru and then living in Oregon, I fell in love with the ocean. With our own family, Jon and I spent summers on the lake with our boat pulling the kids and their friends on inner tubes or wakeboards behind us. Jon gifted me a paddleboard a couple years ago, and I have spent hours being on the water with my paddleboard.

Jon and I discovered scuba diving while living in Saipan. Being underwater is what I imagine flying to be like. Free to move with nothing holding you back, all while discovering a world that is unseen to most. Jon and I spent most of our free time outside our classroom teaching to go diving. With Jon's part time job at a dive shop, we were able to take all the courses on diving we wanted at a reduced price. Throughout all these courses, we learned how to control our movement around the environment, both for our safety, the safety of others, and the safety of the natural habitat we were diving in.

One of my favorite types of diving is drift diving. Drift diving can make one feel a bit out of control but is also exhilarating. This is when one jumps off a boat into a current that is running along the reef. You are instructed to not fight the current, but just go for the ride. It is scary because you realize you cannot swim against the current, as it is too strong. But the boat will be there at the end to pick you up when your dive is done. Divemasters are with you who are familiar with the course and are keeping you safe. What is exhilarating is once you get used to the movement and sensation of not being in control, you are free to take in what is around you. Due to the current, you are surrounded by an abundance of life.

My first drift dive other than Saipan (where I was familiar with the underwater environment) took place in Pohnpei, Micronesia. The emotions I experienced as I descended into the water were ones of terror and panic. But as I saw the divemaster right beside me along with Jon, I was able to relax. The reef wall was absolutely stunning with huge heads of coral. Schools of fish everywhere. I found myself between a large school of barracuda and the reef wall at one point. Sharks were spotted throughout. We saw endless varieties of smaller fish with all the colors you could imagine everywhere swimming around and between the corals, in and out of holes and small caves. We could never stay in one spot observing all the wildlife as the current kept us going. The dive ended on top of the reef wall where we could get out of the current and do our safety stop, finally able to control our movement while enjoying the beauty.

Another drift dive that stands out is a dive we did on the island of Palau, Micronesia. The dive was on "The Blue Corner," which is a well-known spot to divers around the world. By this time, I had more experience with drift dives and was more relaxed. The highlight of this dive was when the current took us to a corner where the reef jutted out and two currents came together. Schools of sharks would be found here as the current brought so much food. I found myself diving with sharks all around. I understand this is not for everyone, but it was thrilling for me.

Other favorite dives have been calmer ones with little to no current: night dives where there is a full moon and you can turn your flashlight off and look around with the moonlight shining through the water. Diving through strands of tiny bioluminescent creatures that fall like curtains around me. Enchanting.

The Impact of Movement on Vision

Another one of the characteristics of individuals with CVI is the need for movement. Movement is something that can be noticed in all visual fields, (meaning all areas of sight including central, upper, lower, and peripheral fields). One does not need to use their central field to be able to perceive movement. One does not need to see details to notice movement. Movement alerts the person to turn towards what is moving. If one catches movement out of one of their peripheral fields, the instinct is to turn towards whatever caught their attention, then use their central field to identify what is moving.

> **Movement alerts the person to turn towards what is moving.**

A child who is deeply impacted by this visual impairment often requires movement to be able to perceive an object. For example, if a stationary item is placed in their visual fields, they may not notice it. Incorporate a little movement into that object, and the student will be more likely to detect its presence. A time may come where movement is no longer needed to recognize the object. It can be seen either stationary or with movement. However, movement may still be required when looking at something in the distance or when a lot of other items are surrounding the object one is being asked to locate. Movement remains an important support and is often needed at some level.

Holy Spirit Movement

When I think of movement in spiritual terms, the Holy Spirit comes to mind. In the Bible, this movement is tied to many properties of water. As we cannot live without water, we cannot live the life God calls us to live without the Holy Spirit. Words in the Bible that associate water with the Holy Spirit include: hovering, flowing, cascading, the act of "being poured out," flooding, overflowing, and even quiet or still waters. The term "living water" is used throughout the Bible referring to a knowledge of God, Jesus, and the Holy Spirit. I love all the different ways water is described in the Bible. It shows the many ways the Holy Spirit interacts with us. No wonder water is involved in being born again through baptism.

Hover

"Now the earth was formless and empty, darkness was over the surface of the deep, and the Spirit of God was *hovering* over the waters" (Genesis 1:2 NIV).

To hover means to stay in one position above something else, waiting. To linger close. In this case, there is expectation as something is happening in this hovering.

Flow

Jesus is found talking to a crowd of people and hinting about the coming of the Holy Spirit in the book of John. "On the last and greatest day of the festival, Jesus stood and said in a loud voice, 'Let anyone who is *thirsty* come to me and *drink*. Whoever believes in me, as the Scripture has said, *rivers of living water* will *flow* from within them.' By this he meant the Spirit, whom those who believed in him were later to receive..." (John 7:37-39 NIV).

To flow means to be able to move from one place to another with ease. Nothing to hinder or stop this flow.

Poured out

"And hope does not put us to shame, because God's love has been *poured out* into our hearts through the Holy Spirit, who has been given to us" (Romans 5:5 NIV).

To pour out means to freely express without restraint, to move in large numbers, giving "your all" while holding nothing back.

Cascade

To flow rapidly in a steady stream. The Passion Translation of this same verse talks about the "endless love of God *cascading* into our hearts" (Romans 5:5 TPT).

To be poured downward rapidly and in great quantities.

Flood

"And I pray that he would unveil within you the unlimited riches of his glory and favor until supernatural strength *floods* your innermost being with his divine might and explosive power" (Ephesians 3:16 TPT).

An overflowing of water beyond its normal confines, especially going over onto dry land.

Overflowing

"Endless love beyond measurement that transcends our understanding-this extravagant love pours into you until you are filled to *overflowing* with the fullness of God!" (Ephesians 3:19 TPT)

Being so full that the contents go over the sides.

Quiet

"He makes me lie down in green pastures, he leads me beside *quiet waters*" (Psalms 23:2 NIV).

To be silent, calm, still.

There is a downside to movement as well. Movement can also distract and take our eyes off what they should be directed at. Movement is all around us, and it is not all from God. Discernment is needed to be able to distinguish between what is God's movement and what is man's. When we pay attention to the movement of man and turn away from listening to the Holy Spirit, we run the risk of quenching His Spirit.

Quench

The Bible has a specific warning concerning this. "Do not *quench* the Spirit" (1 Thessalonians 5:19 NIV).

To extinguish or suppress. We quench the Holy Spirit when we refuse to let Him work through us.

So, how are we to discern? How do we know whether the movement that catches our attention is from God or from man? Paul tells us to think on the following: "Finally, brothers and sisters, whatever is true, whatever is noble, whatever is right, whatever is pure, whatever is lovely, whatever is admirable—if anything is excellent or praiseworthy—think about such things" (Philippians 4:8 NIV). These are what we should be paying attention to. It also helps me to go further and remind myself of the fruits of the Spirit. Some things I pay attention to may appear good in the moment, but the feelings they produce in me create anxiety, jealousy, fear. These thoughts are not from God. Pay attention to how you respond emotionally. Emotions are from God and a tool He uses to communicate with us.

"For the flesh desires what is against the Spirit, and the Spirit desires what is against the flesh; these are opposed to each other... Now the works of the flesh are obvious: sexual immorality, moral impurity, promiscuity, idolatry, sorcery, hatreds, strife, jealousy, outbursts of anger, selfish ambitions, dissensions, factions, envy, drunkenness, carousing, and anything similar" (Galatians 5:17, 19-21 CSB).

The Word is clear about the outcomes of what we will experience if we pay attention to the wrong kind of movement. We get distracted, and this distraction turns us away from God. Here are the emotions, the results of paying attention to what God is doing through the movements of the Holy Spirit in your life.

"But the fruit of the Spirit is love, joy, peace, patience, kindness, goodness, faithfulness, gentleness, and self-control..." (Galatians 5:22-23 NIV).

Movements of the Holy Spirit in Our Lives

I have been on a journey in my own experience with the Holy Spirit learning to recognize the many ways He speaks to me and works through me, His many movements.

My mom likes to tell the story of when I was a little girl and how we were at home in La Paz waiting for my dad to come home. While we were waiting, I spoke up and started praying that God keep my dad safe from getting in a car wreck. When my dad finally came home, he told us how he had almost gotten in a car wreck, but at the last moment, the oncoming car somehow missed hitting him. This didn't faze me at the time. I wasn't paying attention to my prayer or why I prayed it. Dad was home and all was good. Life went on. I didn't understand what was happening to me at the time, but the Holy Spirit was working through me. Age doesn't matter to God. He will partner with anyone to bring about His purposes.

Age doesn't matter to God. He will partner with anyone to bring about His purposes.

I went through a time where I struggled with wondering whether God saw me and noticed me. I didn't believe I was good enough or important enough for Him to use me. I even questioned if He was real.

One morning in my living room while I was praying, I asked God if He was real and how I would know. My right arm started shaking uncontrollably. This began a season where whenever I would worship Him, whether publicly in church or privately, my arm would start to shake. It was a little disconcerting and embarrassing at times, mostly because I was not sure how it would be taken by those standing around me.

I remember the first time my daughter Paige noticed and how she was a little worried. I whispered in her ear that I was okay, I wasn't having a seizure, and that I would explain later. She had tears in her eyes when I told her what was happening. This went on for many months. My faith increased as I experienced God's immense love for me. He knew me so well and that I needed that whole-body experience that included the physical aspect to really believe. Gradually the shaking has decreased, but my awareness of Him being right beside me has increased. The shaking does come on at times when I do still need it or when I am praying for someone. I like to think of it as a sign that He is there for others to recognize as well.

The Holy Spirit will speak to me, giving me a specific word for a friend. A couple of times I have woken up with my arm shaking along with a word and message for someone. The shaking continues while I write as I let the Holy Spirit clarify what He wants to say to this person. Then my arm is calm again. Somehow the writing is legible.

Sometimes I experience the Holy Spirit in other physical ways. A friend once said to me that she sensed the presence of God so strongly around me. I was not aware of this and asked her why she had that sense. I wanted to know as my faith didn't seem as strong as hers and I felt doubt creep in. She told me to stretch my arm up with my hand open and wait. Within a minute, I experienced the sensation of warm oil being poured into my hand down my arm and through my body. I had never felt anything like it before or since. What spoke to me was that God was not mad at me for doubting. He knew me and understood I needed physical affirmation that He was near, like the apostle Thomas needed to see the physical scars on Jesus's hands and feet. A journey in building my faith so I could be at a place where I could "walk by faith, not by sight" (2 Corinthians 5:7 NIV).

Then there are times where the Holy Spirit speaks quietly to me but in just as much a supernatural way. I may be in a situation where I am experiencing great anxiety. He is teaching me to turn to Him during these times and give to Him whatever I am facing. When I take the time to do this, my emotions are transformed, and where anxiety once was, peace takes its place. Where dislike exists for a certain person, compassion and understanding enter in changing my heart. Where situations were once seen as problems, they now are perceived more as opportunities for God to work. The Holy Spirit is on the move!

Countless times the Holy Spirit has worked by dropping ideas into my head when I am working with my students. Ideas come with strategies to try or tools to make that will help a particular student access their environment better, either visually, auditorily, or through touch.

Growing in Your Ability to Recognize Holy Spirit Movement

How might the Holy Spirit be catching your attention? What are His movements like? Spend some time with the Holy Spirit, thinking back over your life, asking Him to show you when He was speaking to you. In the Old Testament, Elijah was told by God that He was going to speak to him that day, so Elijah waited expectantly. As he waited wild things happened on the mountain including a "powerful wind that tore the mountains apart and shattered rocks", "after the wind there was an earthquake", "after the earthquake came a fire" (I Kings 19:11-12, NIV), but the Lord was in none of these catastrophic events. "And after the fire came a gentle whisper. When Elijah heard it, he pulled his cloak over his face and went out and stood at the mouth of the cave" (I Kings 19:13 NIV).

I think many of us have preset expectations for how the Holy Spirit will speak to us. Because He is the Holy Spirit, obviously, He is going to speak in a way that is grand. Right? But He didn't. He spoke in a quiet whisper, which is exactly what Elijah needed at that moment as he was dealing with fear and being pursued by Queen Jezebel to be killed. God knows.

God knows how to get through to us with whatever we are dealing with. But we have to be paying attention and be alert to be able to recognize His voice. Anyone else would have expected God to be speaking through the wind, earthquake, and fire as they were loud and grand events. But Elijah knew when it was God and was able to recognize His voice and come out to meet Him. It's that time, that intimacy with God that it takes to recognize His voice.

God's ability to speak to you is greater than your ability to listen!

When you are discouraged, remember God's ability to speak to you is greater than your ability to listen! So, take heart. Spend that time with the Lord getting to know Him. Learn to recognize how the Holy Spirit moves in unique ways in your life. You are already known by Him and God understands how to get through to you. But you still have a choice to spend time with Him listening to His voice. A choice of whether or not you will open yourself up to His movements in your life. Will you?

Come, Holy Spirit, come.

10

THE PREFERENCE OF COLOR

"For you created my inmost being; you knit me together in my mother's womb. I praise you because I am fearfully and wonderfully made; your works are wonderful, I know that full well. My frame was not hidden from you when I was made in the secret place, when I was woven together in the depths of the earth. Your eyes saw my unformed body; all the days ordained for me were written in your book before one of them came to be. How precious to me are your thoughts, God! How vast is the sum of them!"
(Psalm 139:13-17 NIV)

During college my brother and I were invited to a church to share what it was like growing up as a missionary's kid. We spoke about how we experienced coming from one culture, that of our parents, and being raised in a different culture, with the result of not quite fitting into either. It was as though each country were a certain color. If Bolivia were blue, for example, all the people there would look, talk, and think blue. The United States might be yellow, full of yellow people. We were different. Neither blue nor yellow, we were a mixture of both. We were green.

I am what is now called a "third-culture kid" (a TCK). A TCK is a child who spends their developmental years in a culture different from their parent's culture or the country of their nationality. One grows up having ties to both cultures but not truly belonging to either one. Being raised in a country outside the United States, I grew up with attitudes and beliefs that are different from those who have lived their whole life in the US. I have a different way of thinking and I often view events and situations in what seem like unconventional ways to those around me. This "ability" can be recognized as a strength, but it can also feel lonely and isolating.

My family moved back to the United States for a year the summer before I entered the 5th grade. Someone in our home church gave me a scholarship to attend Girl's Camp. I had only been in the country a week and was going through major culture shock. Within an hour of arriving at camp, the one girl I knew didn't want to hang around me as I was a little "weird." For most of the week the other girls seemed to avoid me. I had a similar experience when we moved back to the US in my junior year of high school. These experiences formed a pathway in my brain that said I didn't belong. It was a very persuasive lie.

Because I looked like other people, they did not realize how much I was struggling on the inside. That feeling of not fitting in persists to this day, although I am now able to challenge it. But back then the sense of not belonging took away my voice. The lie I accepted essentially made me clam up; I didn't easily open up to people. The sad thing is the more attention I gave to the lie, the stronger it grew, adding more lies to the first one. That neural pathway of feeling overlooked grew deeper and stronger. Not only was I worthless, I was a burden to others. This distorted how I perceived things that people said to me or about me. If I wanted to get together with someone and they said they were busy that week, I thought they were finding excuses not to spend time with me. I was always surprised when people did reach out to be with me.

I remembered growing up in Bolivia, where I didn't fit in physically, having blond hair, blue eyes, and white skin, but where on the inside I felt right at home. However, when I returned to Bolivia after living in the United States for many years, I realized I did not completely fit in with the Bolivian culture either. I began to feel like I had no "resting place" or "home" in this world. Different—green—wherever I was.

A good friend of mine, who also relates to being green, shared the lyrics of *It Isn't Easy Being Green* that Kermit the Frog used to sing on *Sesame Street*. It's like living in a yellow country, the US, where people are so colorful with their reds, yellows, and golds, colors that sparkle and flash, while green is the color of ordinary. Dull. Always in the background. Kermit is right: It's not easy being green.

The Need for Color

Along with the need for light and movement, one of the first characteristics of individuals with CVI is that they often have a preferred color. If a child is highly impacted by CVI, they may only be able to see and recognize one color at the beginning. Single-colored items are more able to be processed at this stage versus objects entailing multiple colors and designs. Of all the colors, reds, yellows, and oranges are the most common the retina responds to. However, there are people who don't follow this pattern. I have a student whose color preference is blue, and he only responded to objects that were blue for a long time. He will now regard other colors but continues to have a preference for the color blue. With time and intervention, the hope is that individuals will expand their visual ability to recognize most colors with the preferred color often used as a highlighter.

Tying Vision With Function

As Phase I in CVI involves individuals who have very little visual response, Phase II is when improvement has been made along with an acquisition of visual skills. There is noticeably more visual response to one's environment. In regards to color, we can now take a preferred color and incorporate it in a functional way throughout a child's daily routine. An example of this would be to take a child who is able to see the color red and provide them with a red cup, a red plate, and a red spoon. This draws their attention to their eating tools, and they are better able to understand what they are looking at and what these tools are used for. Alongside this, whereas only being able to see objects with one or two colors in Phase I, these individuals in Phase II now have the ability to identify objects with three to five colors.

The use of color has several functions. It enables a child to recognize what is around them, especially if they cannot process details. Bright colors can be used to help objects stand out. Placing a bright yellow ball amidst an assortment of other colored toys makes that ball pop out so the child can find it. Color can also be used to help highlight something. It can be used in the background to draw the visual attention to what needs to be seen. An example of this is using color to highlight the main ideas in a textbook or where a student needs to fill in a response on a worksheet. A variety of ways color can be used to help draw visual attention can be implemented when working with students.

We Are Each Uniquely Created

Color is one of the characteristics that shows me how we are each uniquely created, largely because I had lived this theme of being green most of my life. I viewed being green as something negative. Being green meant I blended in and was passed over time after time. It has been a journey as God has shown me otherwise.

These first three characteristics involving light, movement, and color remind me of the Holy Spirit and how the Holy Spirit works in our lives. I started thinking, *What if there is something in each of these attributes that plays a part in renewing our minds? Can there be a correlation between these and the replacing and building of neural pathways based on truth?* As we are created in the image of God, it's like we are coming back to Him and His vision for us when we were in the womb.

It has just been in the last few years that I have come to terms with being green. Not only have I come to terms with it but I am also able to see the beauty in who God has created me to be. Now, my favorite thing to find when agate hunting, that happens also to be the hardest and most elusive to spot, are bits of broken translucent green glass among all the rocks. The few bits of green glass mixed with all the beautiful reds, golds, and clear agates make those agates all the more glorious and vibrant in their own colors. It acts like a highlighter. In the same way, those colors also highlight the green glass.

The latter part of Kermit the Frog's song about being green goes on to describe all the good things he has discovered about being green, and that it is, in fact, an important color. Green is the color of growth. It is approachable and makes others feel comfortable. The color green has the ability to do big things. Things as big as the ocean and a mountain and a tree. Kermit comes to the conclusion that he likes being green. He recognizes it as a beautiful color, and it is what he wants to be.

We are all uniquely created. We all have our own color that is beautiful. I once heard a sermon where it was said that it is vital we learn to love ourselves and accept ourselves for who God has created us to be. We were not created to be like anyone else.

Someone out there is counting on you being you!

Learning to accept ourselves as we are is like being in Phase I, along with coming to recognize and appreciate our own color. Once we do that, we are able to move onto Phase II where God is able to use us. The unique giftings He has given us that go along with our color are activated and we become the person He has created us to be. We are able to begin to incorporate the next piece that comes once visual recognition is established. Function. Living out the good works He has called us to.

The Specialness of Your Color

Paul talks about how God chooses the powerless, the foolish, the weak of this world, the insignificant, people who were viewed as nothing to display His greatness (see 1 Corinthians 1:27-28). I remember when I first read these verses and how they spoke to me. I saw this description of myself written out and then reading that despite all that, God chose me! I didn't recognize it at the time, but this was the beginning of my neural pathways being changed, rerouted.

God uses our weaknesses to display His power (see 2 Corinthians 2:12). What are some of your perceived weaknesses? What does God say about them? Could it be you have been viewing them from a worldly lens rather than through the perspective of God? Often what the world perceives as powerless, foolish, weak, insignificant is the opposite of what God sees. God chooses you because of who He made you to be!

Do you see yourself as a color that stands out? That is bright and sparkly? I have a friend who is one of the most colorful and beautiful people I know. She sparkles and shines and stands out. And it is good and right. She was created this way because of what God has called her to do. As people are drawn to her, she draws them to God. She has this ability to somehow take the focus off herself and place it on God. Her life shows how God uses the various functionalities of color as both a way to stand out and also as a way to highlight what is genuinely important.

Maybe you see yourself as a color that is a bit more "hidden." A color that is more muted than sparkly at first glance. I have friends whose colors are a bit softer, who live more in the background, serving others. Their presence brings peace, order, and calmness. Their color acts as a highlighter and support for those around them, whether this be a job, in church, or elsewhere.

I love this quote said by one of the aides in the Netflix series *Madame Secretary* during a graduation ceremony. It refers to living life as a color whose function is to highlight others. "I'm one of those people who work in the dark... In this world of relentless self-promotion, we've all been raised to think that the limelight is the only light worth seeking. But that isn't the case. If I can impart one thing today, a small, simple truth to carry with you, it's this: achievement is often anonymous. Some of the greatest things have been done by people you have never heard of, quietly dedicating their lives to improving your own" (Madame Secretary Season II, Episode 23).

Along with a special color, I believe we are all a mixture of colors that are both made to stand out as well as to be in the background depending on what God is calling us to do at that time, in that situation. Like the progression of going from Phase I to Phase II, we start to recognize the many colors of who God created us to be. It is a process.

God sees all colors. God is the creator of all colors. God knows how to use all colors and how to speak to all colors. The way you are created is not an accident. You were made the way you are on purpose. Ephesians 2:10 talks about us being "God's workmanship." The Passion Translation refers to us as being "God's poetry." You are God's workmanship, created in Him to do good works. God chose you! You are God's poetry.

11

VISUAL LATENCY

"Therefore, brothers and sisters, since we have confidence to enter the Most Holy Place by the blood of Jesus...let us draw near to God."
(Hebrews 10:19-22a NIV)

The first time I showed Sydney a pair of shiny red bells, she appeared to not notice them for about thirty seconds. During this time, they were presented against a black background slowly being moved back and forth with no sound. The red color gave Sydney the visual support she needed to find the bells as she was familiar with this color and preferred it to others. When Sydney found them visually, I jingled the bells and told her what they were. Then I brought my hand to her shoulder and slid it down her arm to her hand where I placed a bell in her palm. Together, we played with this bell, exploring as we held its unique shape, jingled it, and felt the cold metal beneath our hands. I brought both back up to where she could see them again and waited. This time it took less than fifteen seconds for Sydney to find the bells.

Sydney is an amazing little girl who has gone through more challenges in her life than most four-year-olds. She has limited use of functional vision and is considered blind due to CVI. Sydney is also hearing impaired and relies on hearing aids to discern any type of sound. She falls into that extremely low incidence disability category of being deafblind. Limited ability to move her body due to cerebral palsy is a daily challenge, along with controlling the amount of seizures she has. In spite of all these obstacles, Sydney's personality shines through. When feeling well, she is very social and loves to be around people. Sydney's smiles and vocalizations light up the atmosphere. Her amazing parents, siblings, and support worker surround her with life.

One of our main goals is to build skills that will enable communication. Every activity I do with Sydney correlates with this goal. My ultimate objective for these bells was to enhance awareness of movement of her hands and arms. I had sewn the bells on top of gloves with the finger part cut off so Sydney could still feel the materials we were interacting with. After allowing Sydney multiple times to look at the bells, I placed the gloves on Sydney's hands. My intent was to bring awareness through the sensation of the added weight on the top of her hand along with hearing the jingle when her hands and arms moved. We were working on precursor skills to enable her to interact with her toys, which would build up to using communication switches. It's that understanding of the concept of cause and effect to bring about intentional movement.

After Sydney had used her hands and arms to make the bells jingle, I took them off to present them visually to her again. This last time it took less than five seconds for Sydney to notice and fixate on the bells. The time it took her to see the bells continued to decrease each time they were presented after being explored with her other senses. She was becoming familiar with the new object and building neural connections around the concept of bells.

Latency in CVI

Visual latency refers to the time it may take an individual to notice and visually regard an object after it has been presented to them. As CVI is a visual impairment where the visual processing system is impacted in the brain, this response may take longer. It is important to provide the tools necessary to help the individual see the object. This includes using light, movement, and color as needed. It is imperative to keep in mind that seeing is not just locating the object with one's eyes, but also processing what it is and identifying it. Besides providing the tools and supports, repetition and practice play a part in reducing latency. A child who is greatly impacted may require thirty seconds or more before looking at an object. This is particularly true with objects that are unfamiliar and presented for the first time. As familiarity with the object increases, latency time decreases.

Preparing the Way for the Coming of Jesus

One of the biggest forms of latency in the Bible is the period of time between the Old and New Testament when many scholars say God "stopped talking." During the 400 years before the birth of Jesus, we have no record of any word given by God to His people. Prior to the 400 years of silence, God had spoken through certain individuals, like Moses and Elijah. He appointed prophets and judges throughout this time to communicate what the people needed to hear. Then distance developed between God and the people of Israel. Distance not in the sense that God was not present, but the distance in the people's ability to be aware of Him. Latency increased and grew in the inability to perceive God's voice. Latency that ended up extending to 400 years.

So much time had passed, the Jewish people would struggle to recognize Jesus when He came. In order to recognize something, one needs to be familiar with it. The people of Israel needed to remember God's promises of the coming Messiah. God sent John the Baptist to prepare the people for Jesus and to re-familiarize them with the prophecies spoken from long ago. John was called to be a forerunner for the Lord.

"I am a voice of one crying out in the wilderness: Make straight the way of the Lord- just as Isaiah the prophet said... Someone stands among you, but you don't know him. He is the one coming after me... I didn't know him, but I came baptizing with water so he may be revealed to Israel... I didn't know him, but he who sent me to baptize with water told me, 'The one you see the Spirit descending and resting on-he is the one who baptizes with the Holy Spirit.' I have seen and testified that this is the Son of God" (John 1:23-34 CBS).

God in His mercy gave His only Son, Jesus Christ, so we could have direct access to Him. No more latency. No more waiting to be told what God was saying through other people. Since God cannot be near sin, he sent His Son Jesus to be sin for us. No more having to sacrifice animals for one's sins to be able to approach God. The death of Jesus was the ultimate sacrifice so we could each come near to God. God loved us so much He wanted to close the distance so each individual could have direct access to Him.

"For God so loved the world that he gave his one and only Son, that whoever believes in him shall not perish but have eternal life" (John 3:16 NIV).

The Gift of Loneliness

In terms of our knowing God, I think of latency as being more of a distance concept. The less we know of God, the further distant He appears. As we get to know Him, we come to a realization He is closer than we ever knew.

I have come to be more and more aware of God in the ordinariness of life. It takes time to recognize His presence in our everyday living. Even more so, if we are of the mindset that He only shows Himself in grandiose ways, or only speaks through others. For me, this awareness of His daily presence grew through the area of loneliness.

Much of my life I have struggled with loneliness. I always had friends, but I never felt fully known or seen. Although I wouldn't trade how I grew up for anything, being raised as a missionary kid, I never quite fit in wherever we were living. The loneliness didn't really set in until moving back to the United States my junior year of high school and going into adulthood.

I find it so interesting that when we are honestly seeking healing from past wounds, God will take us right to where it hurts most in order to be able to recreate those erroneous neural pathways. Although I was generally an upbeat and happy person, I found my loneliness was growing more prevalent. I often did not want to be by myself because that was when my thoughts would turn negative. I perceived I was always missing out on something.

In the beginning of this last summer with the thought of all this free time ahead of me, I became aware of God wanting to speak. It started through a good friend who was discerning enough to see that something was going on inside me. She had recently gifted me with the word "available." I had been calling friends to schedule times to get together when this friend told me she sensed God wanted me for Himself. The intuition grew that I was to enter into solitude this summer and be available to Him. I stopped making the calls and began to settle in.

I started listening to Graham Cooke's podcasts and sermons. In one of the first ones, I heard him say, "Jesus wants to give you this message that *you are not missing out on anything today, not if you are intentional to spend it with Me.*" It was like Jesus was speaking right to me through Graham. Peace entered my soul, and I began to heal. The truth is that there is no other place I would rather be than in His presence. But I had to be alone for this to happen. I had to experience what I feared most to find meaning in it. Solitude.

Through this solitude and time spent in His presence, I began to discern His hand in my everyday life. I began to recognize all the little ways He shows His love for me. A flower that catches my eye. A song playing on the internet. Words spoken by a family member that affirm me. Having an unexpected quiet moment to myself. A cat jumping on my lap. These may sound like ordinary occurrences. They are. But God is in them. My latency in recognizing His presence was decreasing as my familiarity with Him was increasing.

Drawing Close

In terms of latency, how do you view your relationship with God? Is He a distant being? Do you know Him as your friend? Or is God someone you have heard about but who is not involved in your life? A distant entity? Maybe just another of the many religions man has come up with?

As my student Sydney grew in her familiarity with the bells, her ability to see and recognize them grew quicker. Less latency, or wait time, was required for her to notice them. Similarly, as we increase in our familiarity with God, we are able to recognize His presence in our lives more and more. God speaks to each of us in unique ways. But it takes time to learn to recognize His voice. Spend time in His presence. As you do, the time it takes to become aware of Him decreases. Likewise, the perceived distance between you also decreases. Latency becomes less and less an issue.

As we increase in our familiarity with God, we are able to recognize His presence in our lives more and more.

It is never too late to put your trust in God. To invite Him into your heart to be a part of your life. The Bible says that whoever calls on the name of the Lord will be saved (see Acts 2:21). Christianity is the only religion that does not require works or effort to get to heaven. Put your trust in Him.

"Draw near to God and he will draw near to you" (James 4:8 CSB).

12

VISUAL FIELD PREFERENCE

"For our present troubles are small and won't last very long. Yet they produce for us a glory that vastly outweighs them and will last forever! So we don't look at the troubles we can see now; rather we fix our gaze on things that cannot be seen. For the things we see now will soon be gone, but the things we cannot see will last forever." (2 Corinthians 4:17-18 NLT)

During the latter part of 2022, my friend was led to give me this verse: "You prepare a table before me in the presence of my enemies; you anoint my head with oil; my cup overflows" (Psalm 23:5 CSB).

It genuinely fit the year and all that was before me. I had been asked to do a half-day presentation on my VistaQuest BaseKit at a conference in Washington for Teachers for the Visually Impaired as well as a shorter presentation on the Foundations of CVI. The following month I gave a presentation via Zoom for a conference in Michigan. As the year went on, my VistaQuest BaseKits began to gain ground and I was encouraged to write articles giving the background of the BaseKits addressing how they were created based on how our visual system works. I was also encouraged to start putting together some videos. At first, I said "no" to the articles and videos. I was being pushed too far out of my comfort zone. I felt I needed to breathe and take things more slowly, but after recognizing the need, I went ahead.

These last couple of years have been characterized by fighting my fears and all the "enemies" in my mind. Lies creeped in, telling me that I wasn't good enough. Lies that as soon as my BaseKits were made public, people would wonder what the big deal was. I would be "found out" as being an imposter. Voices in my head would tell me that I should give up. It would be much safer to live life as I had been, keeping quiet and staying in my corner. In the past I had believed those lies. I hadn't matured in my faith to the point where I could see myself as God sees me. Things were changing, though.

Visual Field Preferences

With a child who has CVI, visual field preferences may be very evident. If a child is in Phase I, they will typically only be able to use their peripheral vision, the right or left side of their visual field. As their vision develops, typically the central vision will start to be used. Next the upper field of vision comes into focus, with the lower visual field being the last to develop. The lower field is often unresolved and has the most long-term impact. This affects mobility, being able to move around in one's environment as well as having difficulty seeing objects when they are placed in that field.

Being aware of a child's visual field is crucial as you want to present objects where they can be seen. It is also important to understand that when a child is only using their peripheral vision, they are not taking in details. Try placing an object or something with writing on either side of your head and read it. You will find this is impossible. What you can see out of your peripheral fields is the color of the object you are holding. You can also notice light and movement. Color, light, and movement alert you that something is nearby, drawing your attention.

What you cannot see is detail. You have to use your central vision to make out the details. Your central vision is surprisingly small. It is only 0.35 millimeters in diameter, about two widths of your thumbnail at arm's distance. Children who are in Phase I cannot use their central field, which is where most of us instinctively place objects when presenting them to others. These children cannot see detail, much less process it. When working with someone in Phase I, the focus is on using materials with color where light and aspects of movement are incorporated. This catches a child's visual attention, and then they themselves will naturally turn to look at it, in time, using their central vision. The details may be taken in bit by bit as recognition and neural pathways are being formed.

The Best Place to Sit

My daughter, Paige, loves acting and has been in many theatrical productions. Whenever we go to a performance, she tells us to sit right in the middle of the auditorium. While sitting in the periphery, we may miss something. The center is where the sound is clearest. In this spot we are also able to view the production more easily in its entirety.

Our peripheral fields are the areas where something catches our attention. Then we decide whether we will spend the effort investigating it, or ignore it and move on. Central vision is where we are able to see detail to identify what we are looking at. When one begins using their central vision, their visual skills are developing and maturing. Their visual library is growing, which increases their understanding as time has been spent processing what is being seen.

The last several years have been a growing time for me in my faith. Time spent in His presence learning to listen to God and becoming familiar with the unique way He talks to me. It has changed me. I began to see myself as worthy and loved. During this time as I faced events and things that stretched me, those intrusive lies would come up trying to get my attention. But I was becoming stronger and more discerning in knowing what voice to pay attention to. Where to direct my central vision. I focused on Jesus and remembered who I was and to whom I belonged. My cup overflowed as I was able to overcome time and again those fears and lies that had plagued me for so long.

I find it ironic how the lower visual field is the last one to be resolved, and more often than not, remains unresolved. The phrase "It's right under your nose" coincides with how the lower visual field often remains a challenge for individuals with CVI. This idiom is used to describe failing to notice something that is obvious. It's like trying to figure something out, not realizing the answer has been there the whole time. I used to wonder if God ever gets exasperated with us when we continually fail at recognizing His touch upon our lives because we aren't paying attention. Words are something that has helped me pay more attention to what is right in front of me, that otherwise I would have missed.

I have a thing for words. Sometimes single words come into my head regarding a person or regarding me from what I perceive God saying. My friend, Marie, makes beautiful word cards with watercolor paintings. I love giving these word cards to friends or people who God impresses upon me. I even had a dream where Marie and I went on a picnic. When we found our special spot, we got out our picnic basket and opened it. Instead of food, it was filled with words.

"Like apples of gold in settings of silver is a word spoken at the right time" (Proverbs 25:11 AMP).

On my 50th birthday last year, another friend gave me a gift of 50 words. Each word is written on an index card with a verse reference attached to it. The words represent God's love letter to me and remind me of who I am in Christ. They remind me to keep using my central vision. Very timely in attacking those lies that still pop up every now and then. God has faithfully prepared a feast for me in the presence of my enemies. Right under my nose. Apples of gold. Agates. My cup overflows.

Where Is Your Focus?

What about you? Are you making choices that will lead you closer to God or further away? What is your gaze focused on?

Thinking back to the theater setting, where are you sitting in your current circumstances? Are you sitting right in the middle where you can hear God distinctly? Are you using your central vision focusing on what He is directing your attention to? If not, are things happening in the periphery trying to turn your attention elsewhere? Anxiety, stress, temptation, lust, need for control, greed for power and self-advancement are all examples of what can take our focus away from God. We have the ability to live a life full of peace and goodness, but we have to intentionally and continuously, place our focus on God.

God tells us how to do this in Philippians 4:4-6. We are to give Him our concerns. Tell Him every detail of our lives. As we do this, His overwhelming peace floods our souls. Verse 8 goes on to say we are to "keep our thoughts continually fixed on all that is authentic and real, honorable and admirable, beautiful and respectful, pure and holy, merciful and kind" (Philippians 4:8 TPT). Every thought fastened to the things of God.

There may be times in our life when we do lose our focus on God. The apostle Peter was focused on Jesus when he stepped out onto the water. However, the winds and the waves caught his attention and doubt came flooding in as he paid more attention to the surrounding circumstances than to Jesus in front of him. As his focus shifted, he started to sink. What stands out to me is that as he started sinking, Jesus was right there to catch him. The moment they stepped into the boat, the storm ceased. Because of what Jesus did, Peter's focus was brought back to where it needed to be (see Matthew 14:25-33). God is aware we are but dust (see Psalm 103:13-14). He is compassionate and gentle with us, understanding our weaknesses. God is faithful and present to help us bring our focus back to Him.

What stands out to me is that as he started sinking, Jesus was right there to catch him.

The same friend who gave me the gift of 50 words recently gave a sermon on the two paths that one can choose in life. This verse is often thought of in terms of salvation, but she pointed out how it can also apply to the daily decisions we make.

"Enter through the narrow gate. For wide is the gate and broad is the road that leads to destruction, and many enter through it. But small is the gate and narrow the road that leads to life, and only a few find it" (Matthew 7:13-14 NIV).

The wide and broad path is all about ourselves. It is the easier path to take as it is familiar, comfortable, and predictable. This path does not take much thought. This path is full of selfishness and leads ultimately to destruction, away from God.

Then there is another path, less traveled on. This path reminds me of how small of a field our central vision is, but looking through it is the only way to view all the details that surround us. It is the path God has for you if you choose to follow His lead. It is often not familiar nor comfortable, and hardship may be along the way, but it is the only route to everlasting peace and joy. Choosing this path takes thoughtfulness and intentionality. Ultimately, it will lead you to God, the only way you can ever see your life the most clearly.

13

VISUAL REFLEX RESPONSE

"For God has not given us a spirit of fear, but of power and of love and of a sound mind." (II Timothy 1:7 NKJV)

Fear. My biggest enemy. Fear is caused by the belief that someone or something is dangerous. That something will cause pain and harm. The pain can be physical, emotional, mental, or spiritual. It can manifest itself in many ways. Fear of rejection. Fear of being left out. Fear of being forgotten. Fear of appearing dumb. Fear of not fitting in. Fear of talking in front of people. Fear of saying something that will offend others. Fear of standing out. Fear of letting people down. Fear of failure. Fear of success. Fear of the unknown. Fear of a lack of self-confidence. The list goes on. These were some of the many ways fear manifested itself in my life.

Where did this fear start? My childhood was positive for the most part. It wasn't until my teenage years that I experienced being bullied and made fun of. These instances deeply affected me to the point where fear started taking over a large part of my life. It started to control me by becoming my go-to reflex, supplanting the place where confidence should have been.

During the year 2022 when I was given Psalm 23:5 by my friend, God was inviting me to rewrite those painful experiences from my past. He was asking me to trust Him and to step out in faith. It was a time in my life when I was being continually stretched by God. Looking back, I recognize that in order for God to use me as He wanted, my reflexes had to change. I was living life through a spirit of fear. Fear was my enemy, and it needed to go. This process started out with the decision to obey God in all things. It was that pin-point obedience.

What this actually entailed, I was finding out, was confronting my fears. Confronting my fears and experiencing His faithfulness through letting go and trusting Him.

One of the first things God asked me to do was play the piano in front of friends. In His infinite kindness, God was targeting several instances during my teenage years where I had been asked to do something in school in front of others and made mistakes. Being from Bolivia, I was often clueless about what people were talking about in the United States and I was taken advantage of, being made the brunt of jokes many times without understanding what was going on. I was made fun of by my peers laughing at me and calling me names. This deeply impacted me to the point of being terrified of doing anything public in front of anyone.

Now I love to play the piano but am very aware I am prone to making lots of mistakes. I only play by myself or around family members because of this. So, it was a huge step in trusting God when I felt Him nudge me to play the piano for my friends. I told myself that the worst that could happen would be I would mess up on the songs. And I did. I made a lot of mistakes. What is key is that no one laughed at me. No one made fun of me. Although it was scary, I recognized I was in a safe place, and my friends, as it happens, were touched by my playing.

This experience started the change that would release the hold fear had over my life. I took another step towards confronting fear in deciding I would obey in spite of it. I was told it was okay to not feel confident when asked to do something. This was incredibly freeing.

When I first started public speaking, presenting on CVI and my BaseKit, I was visibly trembling. But it was okay if people saw my nervousness. The change was slow, but when the enemy realized I could no longer be controlled with fear, something inside me was loosened and set free.

From Atypical to Natural

We are all born with natural reflexes that exist to protect the various parts of our body. Concerning our eyes, there is the visual blink response to a visual threat. This reflex of the eye blinking to a perceived threat is the body's way of protecting the eyes against injury. It's to keep the eyes safe in response to something in the environment. We test these responses by touching a child's nose quickly without warning to note if they will blink in response, and then by waving our hand quickly or snapping our fingers in front of a child's face. Depending on the impact of CVI, the responses can vary from having no blink response at all, to having an inconsistent blinking response, to blinking in response to both tests. This response is not something that we can target specifically but is something that naturally resolves itself as other areas of vision are built up.

One definition of typical means "normal," "natural," "to be in character." God wants His nature in us to be our normal. To live life where it is natural to be at peace. Natural to live full of joy. To have a gentle response to circumstances. To be kind, even when others around are unkind. To be patient in all situations. This is meant to be our natural character! Our typical reflex responses to life!

God wants His nature in us to be our normal.

God's intention for us is to respond naturally to life through His power, with His love, accompanied by a sound mind. Fear should have no part in the equation. This natural response to life is a byproduct of having an intimate relationship with God where we are seen and where we are given the ability to see through His eyes whatever life throws at us.

As we grow and walk in unison with God, our reflex responses become more like the person He created us to be, displaying healthy kingdom values in our life. The fruit of the Spirit—love, joy, peace, patience, goodness, kindness, faithfulness, gentleness, and self-control—become more and more our natural reflex responses.

God is fully acquainted with us and recognizes where we lack in these areas. He wants to bring us closer to Him and to be transformed. He wants to target those areas we struggle with the most, submit those reflexes that are atypical, and go against His plan for us. He wants us to allow Him to work to make them the new normal.

My Cup Overflows

Besides walking in obedience to what God has been calling me to do in this process, God has also been speaking to me through dreams. These dreams have been used to warn, guide, and heal me. They have played the role of building in me a sound mind that turns to faith in God instead of turning toward fear. At times, this response is still inconsistent but it's becoming more consistent as I grow in my trust in God. It has been a process and I have come a long way towards growing into the natural reflexes God created me to have.

To help me move past my fears, God gave me a series of dreams that all hit on specific areas. One dream dealt with my fear of not being able to hear from God when I needed to. I had an important decision to make during this time, and through this dream, God gave me clear guidance and peace.

A couple of dreams dealt with the lack of a sense of security while being ambushed. These dreams were very vivid where I was either being attacked or placed in a situation where I was threatened. Danger was imminent in both dreams. But what stood out was that I was never alone. Angels were surrounding me, preventing the danger from ever touching me. I was protected. This reality of being safe was replacing the hold fear had over me in this area.

The story in the Bible that comes to mind is about Elisha opening the eyes of his servant so he could see that they were surrounded by God's army. Fear vanished when he saw that God's army was so much bigger than the human army that was coming to attack them (see II Kings 6). God showed me through the gift of these dreams how I am completely surrounded. And to confirm this, the word I randomly chose from my gift of 50 words the morning after this dream was *surrounded*. Peace flooded my soul. I was safe within God's protection. Even in the most fearful dangerous situations.

Another dream targeted my fear of not fitting in or being good enough. God had a close friend from college interpret this dream to show me how loved and seen I was, even back during college. I was able to recognize that I had been viewing how people related to me through my inaccurate filter of not fitting in, of being overlooked. God was showing me that that wasn't the reality at all. This dream brought a lot of healing to wounds that, if truth be told, I inflicted on myself.

Through this process, God has proved Himself faithful in guiding me back to where I was designed to operate from in the first place. In His gentleness and understanding of me, He has provided all things needed for so much healing to take place. Experiences to replace painful memories, dreams, even a special friendship. A friendship where I could safely work through my fears of rejection, being forgotten, and not fitting in. A friendship where healing replaced these fears and became a safe place for me. My cup overflows.

What Is Your Typical Response?

Are you able to identify what your enemy is? An area of your life where you struggle? A good strategy to gain victory over one's enemies is first to identify them and where they come from. Spend time with the Lord and identify your enemies. As you do this with Him, work on the awareness of Him being present and desiring all things good for you. The Lord has been with me through my process, and He will do the same for you.

God wants to heal you from the very beginning and bring wholeness to your life. In time, your enemies will lose their hold on your life. Ultimately, God desires us to walk in freedom, in relationship with Him. To live in freedom where our natural reflexes are typical, normal, healthy. Where our responses to life, no matter what the circumstances, are characterized by love, joy, peace, patience, kindness, goodness, faithfulness, gentleness, and self-control.

He frees us to walk, not in a spirit of fear, but in power, love, and a sound mind.

14

DIFFICULTIES WITH VISUAL COMPLEXITY

"...Be still, and know that I am God..." (Psalm 46:10 NIV)

Reilly, my eldest son, traveled to Ghana during the summer of 2023. His first solo trip to the grocery store occurred while living in Accra, the capital city. Because of his visual impairment, it was filled with an anxiety close to panic at times. Reilly had been grocery shopping many times in Oregon, but never alone. He always had someone with him to point out where the milk was, or the eggs. He had relied on help from others in these situations.

It was his fifth week in Ghana, and he had moved to a studio apartment where he had his own stovetop and refrigerator. Food is a major stressor for Reilly as he has an undiagnosed sensory disorder. Food has always been an issue for him growing up, and being in a new country with different foods was a big challenge. He was very excited to have his own cooking facility where he could make his own breakfast with what he was familiar with. But he had to go buy the groceries to be able to do this.

Reilly mustered up the courage and walked to the grocery store which was located inside a shopping mall. First, he had to find the

ATM location to get his money. Using his phone, a common low-vision device tool, he was able to zoom in with his camera to find where he needed to go. The next hurdle was getting through the entrance of the mall as the entrance was not straightforward. A guard was signaling to him, but it was beyond Reilly's ability to see. Reilly couldn't use his phone to look at what the guard was trying to tell him since culturally that would have triggered the guard into thinking Reilly was taking an unwelcome picture or video of him. So, Reilly turned around and walked a safe distance away, waiting for a group of people to lead the way inside. As he entered the grocery store, he began to panic because it was very large and way more complex than he was expecting. He walked down several aisles, trying to calm himself down and stifle the rising panic. After a little bit, he was able to find some items, including a bottle of Coke, but was overwhelmed and left without finding all that he had intended to buy.

Several days later, I was talking with him on the phone and he was trying to mentally get himself ready to go back to the store. I encouraged him, saying that it should be a little easier now because the experience as a whole would be less complex. This time he knew where the ATM was and how to get inside the store as well as the general layout. Little by little, it would get better. This is a brief glimpse into his world showing the impact of visual impairment.

Complexity. Reilly's visual impairment doesn't include CVI, but with the complexity of all the items, the unfamiliarity, the array, the different sensory environment, he still struggled. As many of us do with things that are foreign to us.

Complexity

When working with my students with CVI, I have to manage the amount of complexity around them. This helps support their ability to see and process what they are looking at. The less complex something is, the easier it is to process. There are many visual and sensory complexities to overcome with CVI. Complexity can show up in material things. For example, objects that have multiple colors and designs can be in a busy background where a lot of visual clutter makes it hard to find something specific. In the sensory environment, noise, movement, and even physical touch can be distracting. It is difficult to analyze the various expressions of the human face as our faces are incredibly complex. This characteristic of CVI is one that continues to present challenges throughout one's lifetime regardless of what Phase one is in.

One strategy I use to manage complexity is to present objects that are either one to two colors with a simple design. I often find myself being creative and making my own objects as most toys are very busy. Regarding the background, I limit complexity by providing a solid backdrop. A quiet environment is ideal to simplify sensory input. With facial complexity, I want to encourage the child to look towards faces, particularly the face of their parents. Bright red lipstick and red-rimmed light-up glasses are fun, playful ways to support this specific visual behavior.

My ultimate goal is for the child to be able to use their vision in all environments. But I have to work up to that. Once a child can identify a familiar single-colored object, they can move on to a slightly more detailed object that is similar with the addition of two to three colors. Or I may present the same object within an array of other objects to observe if they can pick it out. If the child is successful in using their vision functionally in a quiet environment, I move to a less quiet environment to start to build up their visual ability. This all comes back to how the thalamus works and how it pays attention to what sensory input is the strongest at that time. My goal is to slowly build up and integrate the various senses so they can be processed through the thalamus simultaneously. But when I start working on visual skills in this area, I need to begin by breaking down the complexity.

Removing Complexity

We live on a rather unique piece of property. It is in the country, on a hill surrounded by forest. Our water supply comes from a spring that is located about three fourths of a mile up the hill. The water flows down a pipe and fills our two 1,500 gallon tanks. During the time of the year when it rains a lot here in Oregon, the water literally rushes down like a waterfall from the spring. During the summer that water path is dry, but the spring continues to produce as it comes from deep down in the earth. Because a continuous supply of water comes into our tanks at all times, they are usually full.

However, there are times when we cannot access our water. This could be because our tanks are empty due to a sprinkler that was inadvertently left on during the summer months or a winter storm that occurred where a tree fell over the pipe, cutting off the flow from the spring to the tanks. There have also been times where our tanks are full, but a broken piece in the operating system in the pump house caused a malfunction to occur, preventing the water from coming to our house.

Complexity—trying to figure out what the problem is. Complexity of the forest after a storm and finding the broken pipes, cleaning the mess of fallen branches and leaves around the spring, or replacing the broken pieces in the pump house. As the problem is discovered, complexity is broken down, and water is able to flow once again.

Simplifying Our Lives

How does complexity relate to our spiritual lives? Maybe, like Reilly during his shopping trips in Ghana, what is ahead of you appears unclear. It may be hard to ascertain the next step to take. Hard to make decisions when the outcome isn't clear. All you realize is that you have to keep moving forward. You can't stay where you are. As Reilly stepped back and waited for others to come to help guide him into the store, maybe you need to take a step back and seek the counsel of others. Listening to someone you trust outside the circumstances can help bring clarity to whatever it is you are facing. A way to help break down the complexity.

The tanks can represent our relationship with God, the time we spend in His presence and get filled. The more filled we are, the more likely we are to overflow. But what about those times we spend in His presence and still struggle? Still question if we are able to hear Him? Or if we have been praying about a particular situation, a particular friendship but not getting clarity... It's that "being in the desert" experience. Is something blocking the flow of recognizing His voice, like the old pump pieces blocking the flow of water from coming into our house? Are we viewing our situation through a filter that doesn't reflect his reality? Spend time in His presence asking Him to help break down the complexity. This can bring clarity and the ability to hear His voice amidst all the chaos. I believe having a Sabbath rest is about dealing with the complexity. Spending time with the Lord in rest can be that baseline of peace that we can come back to in times of crisis.

Complexity can show up in a multitude of ways. This can be through the busyness of life. Work, activities our children are involved in, our own activities, keeping up the home, hobbies, church, etc... At what point do we need to start simplifying our schedules? Learn how to say no to a few things? Are we so busy we don't have time to spend with God?

Complexity can show up in how we think. Is our mind consumed with how we appear to others and striving to look a certain way? Or are we so caught up in legalistic thinking, where we are focusing more on what we should or shouldn't do, on what others are doing or not doing, than on knowing God? I once heard it said, "The greatest reality in your life is the love of God. If you are not aware of it, you are aware of too many other things" (author unknown).

"The greatest reality in your life is the love of God.
If you are not aware of it,
you are aware of too many other things."

Maybe you are having trouble recognizing what is familiar because you are surrounded by the unfamiliar. This can bring on a tremendous amount of anxiety. Take a deep breath and anchor yourself with something familiar. As Reilly found familiarity in the Coke bottle that is universal, it brought a certain amount of comfort, of security. Although he didn't find what he wanted in his first trip to the grocery store, he gained a measure of familiarity with the store, which helped break down some of the complexity for his next go around. Don't give up. Take note of the little victories you have already accomplished. It will get easier as familiarity increases and complexity decreases.

Psalm 46:10 says to "Be still and know that I am God." This is one of my favorite verses because it reminds me of what is important.

"Be still and know that I am God."

"Be still and know that I Am."

"Be still and know."

"Be still."

"Be."

Cutting down the complexity.

15

DIFFICULTY WITH DISTANCE VIEWING

"Draw near to God and He will draw near to you." (James 4:8 CSB)

Paige is what is called a "glass child", a child that in one sense is invisible. You can see right through them, as in looking through glass. A glass child is a term given to someone who has grown up in a home with a sibling who has disabilities and high needs. The glass child is often overlooked due to all the attention placed on the sibling, both from the parents and others.

Without Jon or me realizing it, Paige began experiencing this from the moment we were told our youngest son Peter was blind. As Peter's needs became more and more prevalent with the additional diagnosis of autism, our oldest son Reilly appeared to be losing his vision. We became involved in a medical study on both boys as the combination of their visual diagnosis was considered rare. Twice a year we were traveling up to Portland for testing.

Paige was left in the background throughout this time, seemingly forgotten, while the boys were in the foreground of our attention and time. These trips, along with increased services for the boys, continued for the next five to six years, taking Paige through elementary and into middle school.

Paige has always come across as self-reliant and independent. This, I discovered, is one of the characteristics of a glass child. Jon and I did not realize how much she was hurting as her struggles were unseen. Her worst years were in middle school when we had no idea she was involved in self-harm and on the verge of thinking about ways to take her life. Paige's sense of self-worth and value were greatly diminished. Reilly was going through a hard time and experiencing his own depression. With our belief that he was possibly going to lose his vision, we were not at all focused on Paige. Also at the same time, Reilly was beginning to emerge in his musical gifting. He was given a lot of attention. I think him having a disability with this gifting added to all the attention from friends and family. Everyone was amazed at what Reilly could do. Paige was left behind in the wake of this attention.

This is one of the main regrets I have as a parent, but God is so gracious. In the years since then, Paige has opened up to us. I have asked for forgiveness, and we have spent many hours talking and listening, tears followed up with healing. Paige is a fighter like me, and has emerged in her own gifting with acting, music and leadership. But the years took a toll on Paige and left their mark; neural pathways formed from these experiences. For a time, Paige was not sure she believed in the existence of God. I spent many hours praying over her as did her grandparents and others.

At this time I had been growing in my own faith and felt compelled to start sharing with Paige. I remember the first time I talked with her about how the Holy Spirit had been working in me. Tears formed in her eyes as she said she wanted to know God like that. Looking back, I recognize how prayer as well as certain individuals speaking truth into Paige during this time made a difference.

My co-worker, Barbara, had started experimenting with photography, and we spent many days with her taking photos of Paige, which are pretty incredible. Endeavors like this helped Paige see her worth. Recognizing her innate value has helped Paige grow into an incredibly compassionate and empathetic person, as is often the case with children who are raised in a household where there are siblings with disabilities. It has been one of my greatest joys to watch this process with Paige and have her emerge with so much strength.

The glass child syndrome is a real thing. The families I work with who have other children without disabilities constantly battle this. Guilt is a familiar companion to one not able to be a present parent to all their children. The reality is that a choice to spend time with the other children without disabilities may not always be an option since those who have such high needs cannot be ignored. This is especially the case for parents who have children with high medical needs.

If you are a parent who experiences this, or know someone who does, I encourage you to be kind. Be kind to yourself and forgiving. If possible, ask for help from family and friends to come alongside to help care for your child with disabilities so you can spend one-on-one time with your other children. Acknowledge and validate their feelings when they want to talk with you. If feasible, include them in taking part of their sibling's care. Encourage and support their own individual interests. By doing this, you are giving them the message that they are just as important as their sibling. If possible, connect with other families who may be living with similar issues. Above all, make sure to give yourself a lot of grace throughout this season of raising your children.

Complexity With Distance Viewing

For individuals with CVI, seeing objects at a distance can be challenging. This isn't necessarily due to acuity issues or being near-sighted. It's more of a complexity issue. If you hold the cover of a book a foot away from your face, it is going to take up most of your visual field. However, if that book is presented six feet away, the complexity increases as the surrounding items in the environment also enter the visual field. The further away the object presented is, the higher the complexity with other aspects entering the visual field. For a child with CVI, they may simply not be able to identify or process something presented in the distance.

To be able to identify something from a distance, one needs to first be familiar with it up close. A strategy to help the person pick out a familiar object in the distance is to combine that object with color, light, and/or movement. It is easier to see a bright color that stands out, or something that is lit up, or moving.

One of my strategies with the boys, specifically with Reilly during his soccer games, was to wear a bright yellow rain slicker so he could spot me in the distance. He knew what to look for as he was familiar with the slicker, and the bright color stood out.

Knowing God Personally

The boys' visual issues were so prevalent growing up that that is where we focused for a number of years. And this was necessary. Paige was kept at a distance throughout this time. Amidst the complexities of what was going on with the boys, we lost sight of her. When Jon and I realized what was happening, we were able to change course and with intentionality draw near to her as well.

A major part of drawing near to Paige was conveying to her her own worth and value. I knew the true meaning of this could only come through experiencing God's love personally. I talked a lot to Paige about how much God loved her. During these early times, she had not yet experienced this for herself and I spent a lot of time praying that she would experience this love firsthand. I am always amazed at how God knows us so thoroughly and speaks to us in ways we can understand. He did this in such an incredible manner for Paige.

Jon and I had gone on a diving trip to Honduras the summer of 2022 with the two older kids. Peter does not care for swimming or diving in the ocean and instead opted for personal one-on-one time with Grandpa and Grandma. The trip was a combination of celebrating

Reilly's high school graduation and Paige's upcoming graduation as Covid had disrupted our original plans.

One of Paige's favorite animals in the ocean are the rays, especially the eagle rays. They can be spotted for about 30 seconds or less in the distance. On our last dive, I prayed that it would be an extra special dive where God would show Paige in some way how much He loved her. Paige and I chose to dive around a shipwreck surrounded by a sandy bottom where rays were most likely to be observed. Jon and Reilly were off exploring the reef wall nearby.

As Paige and I were checking out a side of the wreck, I spied a large stingray buried in the sandy bottom with the tip of his tail sticking out. We watched him shake himself out of the sand and go off into the distance. At this time, we both turned our gaze up and there was an eagle ray about ten feet away moving slowly, watching us. It was as if he was inviting us to pursue him. We ended up following this eagle ray for about 10-15 minutes with no one else around. The eagle ray stayed at this same distance from us, no further. He circled the wreck with us close behind. He even went down into the sand for a sand bath and came back up, all the time keeping his eyes on us. It's like he was showing off precisely for Paige and me. It was only when some other divers showed up that the eagle ray went away into the distance. It was an incredible experience.

When we rose to the surface, the first thought that came to my mind was how much God loved Paige. I shared with her my prayer prior to the dive and how God knew exactly what would bring her delight. We have matching stuffed eagle rays on our beds to help us remember this amazing, personal, up-close encounter showing God's love. An altar of remembrance.

Finding God in the Distance

Many of us go through times in our lives with the impression that God is distant. This arises for various reasons regardless of how long one has walked with the Lord. This can occur due to not being familiar with God in the first place, or during complex life situations where our faith may be challenged. But to be able to recognize God from a distance, or in a complex situation, one needs to be familiar with Him up close first. To know Him and have a relationship with Him.

Elijah is one of my favorite biblical characters. His life is a good example of how God can be found in the distance, both in stepping out in faith and also when one's faith grows weak due to life circumstances. It is clear Elijah cultivated a relationship with God. His story starts out describing him as "standing in the presence of God" while talking to King Ahab. As you read, you can see that God spoke to Elijah, and Elijah listened and obeyed. Their relationship was close.

One of the most well-known stories of Elijah has to do with him setting up an altar of the Lord with a bull sacrificed on top of it and somehow drenching it with water in the midst of a drought. God's power was demonstrated plainly to the people when He came down and consumed the sacrifice, including the drenched altar. Because Elijah operated from a close relationship with God, his faith was strong and persistent. He knew who God was and from this knowledge was able to step out in faith.

After the event with the altar, Elijah knew it was time to end the drought and went up a mountain, bowing low to the ground and praying with his face between his knees. An act of intercession.

Elijah had faith that God would continue to follow through and answer his prayers for rain. He persisted in prayer and kept telling his servant to look in the distance. At first, nothing could be seen as he started praying, but he persisted with the awareness that God was going to act and bring about rain. This intercession resulted in a huge rainstorm that ended the drought (see I Kings 18).

What stands out to me after these two incredible events is that Elijah lost his faith temporarily. In the complexity of the situation, Queen Jezebel was determined to kill him for challenging her gods, and he fled in fear. In a sense, he created distance between himself and God by running away. Distance that was in his mind, but not reality. I love how God met him where he was throughout this time and provided for his needs. His physical needs were met as well as his mental, emotional, and spiritual needs. God brought him to a place where the complexity was taken away and Elijah could once again be aware of God's presence in the simplicity of being hidden and quiet. God brought Elijah close to him so he could commune with him (see I Kings 19). God spoke to him in a gentle whisper one could only hear if one was near.

Drawing Near

Have you had a time when life was so hard that you lost your faith for a while? Lost sight of God's hand on your life? The reality is God has you in His hand. When it feels impossible to draw close to Him, He draws close to you. Can you recognize Him in these instances?

It is understandable how God can come across as distant if one has not had a personal experience with Him. Like Paige, once we start having these personal encounters, we begin to recognize how near He is and how involved He is in our lives.

During the crucifixion, even Jesus felt the apparent absence of God. You can grow in your relationship with God so that your faith holds you even if you cannot perceive Him. Faith in the midst of complex circumstances, where you are familiar enough with God to trust that He is working.

As we become more intimate with Him, we are better able to recognize Him from a distance.

We all need to experience God in our own way. Like Paige, we need to be able to bridge that distance to believing in God for ourselves through personal encounters with Him. To have Him be near and present with us. As we become more intimate with Him, we are better able to recognize Him from a distance. To be able to recognize Him in the midst of life's happenings. Reilly knew to look for that yellow slicker when he wanted to find out if we were present. Do you know what to look for to recognize God is present?

Are you conscientiously drawing close to Him? As you do, the distance between you and God will decrease.

16

DIFFICULTY WITH VISUAL NOVELTY

"My dear brothers and sisters, take note of this: Everyone should be quick to listen, slow to speak and slow to become angry..." (James 1:19 NIV)

Before starting to write this book, I was led to read a book by Patricia King called *Live Unoffendable*. King said that the year 2020 was like this spirit of offense had fallen on the country. It brought about so much disunity, predominantly in the church.

Prior to 2020, I had been meeting every Thursday after work with my close group of friends. Our purpose was to grow together in our love for the Lord and encourage one another. With the onset of all the issues that were brought up in 2020, I felt a division growing in my heart; I viewed various things differently than others in the group. I never voiced these sentiments but chose to be offended in my spirit. It affected me to the point where I stopped attending the group for many months.

Patricia King showed me how being offended is something that is a choice. But be aware that if you choose to take offense, it comes with a lot of extra baggage: anger, bitterness, judgment, unforgiveness, and pride. I didn't necessarily experience these towards my friends, but I recognized the enemy tempting me to go down that road. Through God's grace and recognizing how much goodness was in that group, I gave it to God. He helped me appreciate that their perspective and beliefs also came from a place of wanting to follow Him. I returned and am so thankful as they are one of the greatest blessings in my life.

Fast forward to the summer of 2023. I had invited the group to my home for an afternoon of being together. As I was getting ready and cleaning up the living room I browsed over my bookshelf and started becoming nervous. This was the first time for several of the women to come to my home. What if they saw what I read and were offended?

Full disclosure, I have books from all sorts of people, not all popular with some of my friends. I have many books by various theologians and authors that I admire like Brennan Manning, Pete Greig, Chuck Perry, and Greg Boyd. I also have many books from various other leaders who I learn from like Barack Obama and his wife, Michelle. I read his book *The Audacity of Hope* when he was running for president as I wanted to understand more about him. I found myself relating to him on a personal level, especially with how he grew up, living overseas and coming back to the United States. His own spiritual experience with the Lord and being baptized touched me as well as his heart for people and their struggles.

I have all these books from various points of view because I have a desire to understand as many sides of a topic as possible. To recognize the good in both sides as well as the bad. I used to think this open-minded approach was negative as I would be swayed from side to side as I explored. However, I now identify this as a strength. I believe there are always two sides to something, and often truth to both viewpoints.

Even though this tactic has worked for me, I still felt anxious not knowing if I would receive judgment from others who don't believe the same, in particular from this group that I value so much. But then it hit me that resisting being offended works both ways. I was first offended by what they believed, and now I was scared they would be offended by me, which is still an offense! I can't manage others' perspectives of me; I can only manage myself. With that, I surrendered my emotions to God once again and decided to trust Him no matter what the outcome was.

It is so easy to tend to judge those who think differently from us. One of the things that Greg Boyd emphasizes in his teaching is that all humans have inherent value because we are all created in the image of God. We are going to run into people who live in a way we do not agree with, who have viewpoints and opinions we do not share. Regardless of what we think, this does not change their value. If we are not given the privilege of knowing someone else's story, we would do well to withhold judgment, instead choosing to recognize their inherent worth.

Difficulty With the Unfamiliar

People with CVI have difficulty seeing things that are unfamiliar. Without a neurological connection related to something familiar, they will not be able to process what they are looking at. I can present a brightly colored toy in front of a child, but if it is new to them, there may be no recognition or behavior showing they even notice the toy. Now I can get a very different response by bringing in a familiar toy they play with every day. This toy they will turn towards, see, and respond to.

Envision yourself in a crowded cafeteria. In walks a person dressed up in a dinosaur costume. Those of us with typical vision would stop what we are doing and look toward the person in the dinosaur costume. It would capture our attention because it is different and stands out. However, for the individual with CVI, their response may be the opposite. They would most likely turn away from the dinosaur or appear to not notice it at all.

When a child is deeply impacted, there will be little to no visual curiosity in unfamiliar environments. As everything is new around them, they have no anchor to tie the information to, no neural pathways to build upon. The way to progress through this characteristic is to build upon neural pathways that already exist, working with what is familiar and then steadily branching out.

To help my students accept new perspectives, I am strategic with my approach. When I am making a visual calendar of the school day for my students who have the ability to identify and process 2D pictures, I start by taking the pictures from their perspective. I take a picture of the area of the room where the reading group occurs. For recess time, I take a picture of the swing, a favorite activity of one of my students during this time. To take these pictures, I have to squat to be at the same eye level of my students sitting in their wheelchairs. I have found that when I take the picture standing up from my perspective, they may not comprehend what they are being shown.

The first time I noticed this was when I took a picture of the music note outside the music classroom of one of the schools I go to. I was standing and clicked the picture head-on. My student at the time did not understand what the picture stood for. So I bent down to look at the music note to ascertain if it would appear different from the picture I took. It did. I took another picture from that lower position, and my student now understood the visual picture symbolizing it was time for music class.

We need to do the same with each other. Listen and look at a situation from each other's perspectives to accurately understand the other person's thoughts.

God Loves Diversity

We naturally gravitate towards people who are like us. People with whom we have similar opinions, hobbies, professions, race, political leanings, gender, etc... Ways of thinking we are familiar with and can understand. It's easy to stay within our known group because they are safe with less chance of conflict occurring. However, we all have inherent value and are all created in the image of God.

I find people who love God in all walks of life. People who have different viewpoints than I do, whether these be ideological, political, or of life in general. I believe growth occurs when, instead of focusing on our differences, we pursue our shared characteristics. Focus on the shared love of God, on love of people. I have found that as I branch out and get to know people from all walks of life, I can recognize their beauty, their value. I appreciate how God works through them in their corner of the world. Even with those who think differently from me. There is value in diverse thinking.

God approaches diversity in the Bible in many instances. One of these takes place when the first church comes together after Pentecost described in the beginning of Acts. Three thousand people put their faith in God, gave up their possessions and lived together as they grew in their faith. I assume these people came from different walks in life. From different political parties, different ways of thinking, different countries, languages, family backgrounds, and cultures. Yet they were bound together in love and common purpose. Unity. Another instance of God working through diversity is the story where God gives Peter a vision preparing him to go spread the Gospel to the Gentiles. This vision equips Peter to expand his thinking to where he will not take offense or offend the people he is being called to (see Acts 10:9-15).

One story that has always stood out to me is the story of Matthew and Peter in the Bible. They were the first two disciples Jesus chose, and it so happens they possessed two politically different mindsets. Yet they were both equally called to follow God. I love how in the book of Matthew, as he recounts the moment Jesus was betrayed, he doesn't identify Peter as the one who cut off the ear of the slave of the high priest. Matthew just says "one of the disciples." We read from the book of John, this disciple is identified as Peter. By not naming him in his book, it appears that Matthew was trying to protect Peter. What a beautiful picture of friendship. Despite the differences in their backgrounds, the difference in their ways of thinking, their common love for Jesus united them, creating a strong bond of friendship and loyalty.

Seeing From Different Perspectives

Through my journey of discovering how seen I am by God, I find that I am more able to see others. To regard others as God regards them. Whereas I may have been quick to react and be offended, I am now more able to discern the reason for the actions or opinions of the other person. Instead of choosing offense, a desire to understand takes its place.

It's important to take time to become familiar with our own perspective, including a comprehension of why we think the way we do. I have found with myself that I have at times discovered I was looking through incorrect filters. Humility and a desire to learn, even when it may highlight our own shortcomings, is where growth occurs.

When you come across differences in opinions or differences in approaching situations, how do you reconcile those differences? Do you attempt to consider looking from the other person's perspective? Do you take the time to listen to their story? When you do this, do you gain a new understanding of the situation?

The culture of the world, and sometimes even the church, promotes an "us/them" mindset. How do we get past this to the point where we strive to understand each other, in spite of differences? As we operate from the belief that all have inherent value, our response to others becomes missional.

As we operate from the belief that all have inherent value, our response to others becomes missional.

Referring back to my students, when they understood what the pictures I took represented, I was able to take pictures of the same objects from different viewpoints. Through these various viewpoints, my students gained a much broader understanding of what the object or concept in the picture was. If it was a car, they learned what the car looked like from different angles. It was still the same car.

What if we could apply this same principle when working with people we may disagree with? Maybe if we listen, we could get a broader understanding of whatever the disagreement was over. At the same time, we are upholding the inherent worth of each person.

When I don't understand something, I have tried to research both sides of the issue. I have read biographies or books written by people who believe differently, but who believe in God and love God. I may not always end up agreeing with their conclusion, but I do find I develop a greater understanding and appreciation for that person. By taking the time to learn their perspective, doors open for more conversations, more dialogue. This process can be painful but also one of great growth. The Holy Spirit moves when we show we are willing to be open and learn.

I encourage you, as you join us all on this journey to see and be seen, to think about the perspectives you have that may not be complete. Hold onto your core convictions, but do as my students do and consider branching out to view the topic from various facets. This may be by reading books on other religious or political perspectives, engaging in a conversation with someone who you considered ignorant, or asking God to show you more about something.

God understands our humanness and the way we think. He calls us to follow Him, and this always involves drawing others to Him. We are human, and we will be offended by others from time to time. What is encouraging is how God prepares the way, just like He did with Peter, for what He is calling us to do.

17

ABSENCE OF VISUALLY GUIDED REACH

"Therefore, since we are surrounded by such a great cloud of witnesses, let us throw off everything that hinders and the sin that so easily entangles. And let us run with perseverance the race marked out for us,"
(Hebrews 12:1 NIV)

In 1993, I competed in the NAIA Track and Field Nationals in the Women's Racewalking event and finished 11th in the nation. It was a relatively new sport at the time, and I was the only woman competitor from my school, George Fox College. The reason I started racewalking was mostly to spend time with my brother, who had already competed at the national level the previous two years. My brother and I had a close relationship growing up, and that year going on three to four-hour walks with him was priceless.

During my middle and high school years in Bolivia, I was always the last pick for teams during PE class. The team that got stuck with me would groan when my name was finally called. It took away whatever confidence I might have had. As a result, I played horribly, whether it was soccer, basketball, or volleyball, always missing the ball. This had a long-lasting profound effect on me. To this day, I shy away from participating in team sports, afraid I am going to let the team down.

God has a way of bringing the right people at the right time in our lives. Anita, my best friend from childhood, has taken me under her wing and spurred me on to face my fears during different seasons of my life. She encouraged me to try out for the cheerleading team during my senior year in high school in the US, spending hours helping me get ready. She knew I struggled with confidence. It was a gift from God to be a part of this team after feeling ostracized by my classmates in my school in La Paz.

Later on in life, it was Anita again who pushed me to pick up running. I was still struggling with my lack of self-confidence. Anita knew I needed to do something to pull me out and bought me a whole wardrobe of running clothes to get me started. I was in my early 40s when I started running. Participating in races, including half marathons, a full marathon, triathlons, and relay team running events, has been a part of my life ever since. God knew I needed to do something challenging in a tangible way to make my brain align with my body.

As I ran and participated in races, I was teaching myself I could do hard things. My confidence was being built up, physically erasing those painful neural pathways from my past. As time passed and wounds healed, another reason to keep running replaced this one. Relationship. I have made several close friends through running over the years.

In 2023, I took the plunge and started VistaQuest, my own business targeting families and educational teams who work with children with CVI. I found myself speaking at several conferences. I felt covered and like I was where I needed to be, but sometime in the spring of 2023, my confidence plummeted and doubt crept in. I felt fear of what others would think, wondering if I had something worthwhile to share. All these fears started taking over. I was being pushed out of my comfort zone. I needed another realignment of my mind. It was also the year I turned 50. Anita and I had promised each other years ago that we would do a triathlon together when we turned 50. Good timing as I needed to start training and believing in myself again, believing I was who God said I was.

Anita had not planned to come home during the summer of 2023. We decided to still do the triathlon, even though we couldn't do it together. However, she surprised me and showed up in Oregon! During the time she was in Oregon, no official triathlon competition was scheduled, so she set one up for us herself. It was an unexpected gift from God through Anita. It demonstrated to me how well He knows me and how important this was for me to do this with her in person.

The Alignment of Physical Response to Vision

This last characteristic of vision is unique from the previous nine in that it happens after the first part of visual processing takes place in the brain. It involves the follow-through and what physically transpires as a response to what one is seeing. Visually guided reach is about bringing the visual response together with the motor response.

The absence of visually guided reach refers to the inability to look and reach at the same time. This is often observed in children with CVI as they have difficulty processing what it is they are seeing. A child will look at an object, turn away, and then reach for the target while continuing to look away. It is too much information for the brain to combine what is being looked at in addition to figuring out where it is in space to accurately reach for it. These are two separate processes we don't realize our brain is doing all the time. This behavior of looking away can be misinterpreted as disinterest. But if given adequate wait time, the child may show interest and reach for the object. Time is needed to process and respond. With the CVI supports in place (incorporating color, movement, light, and breaking down complexity), a child may be able to look and reach simultaneously for an object, which ultimately is the end goal. When an individual does not have the ability to reach or use their arms, the focus is on being able to look at what it is one is touching while interacting with it. It is all about the visual processing taking place in the brain so the workings of the physical body align and work together.

Coming Into Alignment

We are created to function as whole beings. This includes the physical, spiritual, mental, and emotional parts of who we are. All working together simultaneously. No part separate, but all coming together as one person. It is scientifically shown how synaptic connections are made through neurons creating new pathways as our bodies move.

Paul tells us in Romans to present our bodies as a living sacrifice. What is enlightening is that the verse after this talks about the renewing of our minds (see Romans 12:1-2). In my experience, I have found healing and a realignment of my neural pathways as I step out in faith physically doing something challenging. God has enabled me to heal from past wounds, exchanging fear for trust and peace through my running.

The fear of being left behind is one of the fears that has haunted me. My last half marathon targeted this fear. It was the summer of 2022, and the day started out as every runner's nightmare. My running partner and I had picked up our packets the night before and had a perfect meal loaded with carbs. Everything was all set from the time I would get picked up to how long it would take us to get to the race. However, I set my alarm to go off at 4:45, not realizing it was set for pm, not am.

When I woke up that morning, it was light outside, and I immediately knew something was wrong. The clock said 6:11 am. The race was set to start in forty-nine minutes. My phone showed dozens of missed calls and texts. We have no doorbell and our dogs were inside, so I was never alerted. I barely had time to use the bathroom and throw my clothes on, but I made it out the door in five minutes.

I won't tell you how fast I drove down the highway. Let me just say it was good no police officers were around. The last bus to pick people up was at the parking lot, and a few runners were sprinting to get on the bus. I made it to the race as they were singing the national anthem. It took me two miles into the race to catch up to my running partner. By this time, I had calmed down a bit and was acutely thankful for having made it. I ran well the next six miles and then hit a wall. The last five miles, I was dry heaving, and it was all I could do to keep going. I realized with my family out of town, no one knew what I was doing or could help me if something happened. I have a history of severe migraines, and it was prime conditions for one.

But something happened during the last mile that made this one of my best races. I came upon a young woman who was in worse condition than I was. I caught up to her and asked how she was doing. A lot of curse words came out, which, to be fair, I was also thinking in my brain in regard to my own situation. She told me her toes were bleeding and one leg wasn't working right. I told her I would stick with her and we would finish together. As we ran, this woman told me it was her first race and that she hadn't trained for it. No one was present cheering her on. We finished together providing mutual support for one another, and that was the last I saw of her.

This woman taught me a powerful truth. One of my fears came to pass where I was literally left behind. But because I was left behind, I found out God was still right by my side. He never left me. Through what I thought of as being left behind, I was able to be present for this woman in her time of need. It was a breakthrough for me, and this fear has since been replaced by the knowledge that when I am living alongside God, I will always be where I am supposed to be. I may not see the whole picture at the time, but I trust that God knows exactly what He is doing. What could have been one of my worst races ever turned out to be one of my most memorable.

When I am living alongside God, I will always be where I am supposed to be.

When I find myself finishing a race, something inside me shifts. Something aligns as it was meant to be aligned. Synaptic connections are firing away, creating new neural pathways as old fears are overcome. Former patterns of thinking of myself as a failure become weaker and weaker. I am now an overcomer. Once again, new courage enters into my soul.

Running Our Race

It is significant that a number of verses in the Bible refer to us training as athletes. Verses that talk about disciplining our body like an athlete, how not to be disqualified from a race, and to running our own race with perseverance. A race that is marked out for us. We are to run in such a way as to get the prize (see Hebrew 12:1 and I Corinthians 9:24-27).

When I first started running, I had to train my muscles and work through the pain. Ironically, I am not one of those runners who enjoys running. I struggle. I have noticed on exceptionally long races, the last part feels like it could go on forever, like the remaining distance somehow triples.

There are similarities with our spiritual lives. When we first come to the Lord, it can be hard to get into the practice of spending time each day in prayer talking with God and reading our Bible. As we exercise these new muscles, we start to recognize His voice more often and this time becomes something we look forward to. Then there are times and situations where we need God's touch as we are going through something difficult. Often right before that breakthrough to the "finish line", the battle seems to get worse. Like the end of the race. I have found that when my confidence is low yet again, and my fears and anxieties are heightened, it is almost always before something significant happens. All the more reason to keep persevering and running so I don't miss the prize.

Where are you currently in your race? Are you at the beginning of training where you are learning how your spiritual muscles work and how to be disciplined in using them? Are you further in the training phase where God is working at realigning broken mindsets, healing wounds from your past? Or are you in the race heading toward the finish line, where you are pouring out your heart, soul, and body to get that prize? Don't give up.

What if we honestly believed that God is for us and not against us? That He has a plan for each of our lives that fits? A race that he has prepared specifically for each of us? When we believe this, we are able to make the changes needed in our lives. God will provide the strength for the next step if it aligns to his will. "Now to Him who is able to [carry out His purpose and] do superabundantly more than all that we dare to ask or think [infinitely beyond our greatest prayers, hopes, or dreams], according to His power that is at work within us..." (Ephesians 3:20 AMP). I am convinced through personal experience that when you step out in faith, you will be surprised by what God has in store for you and the prize He has waiting for you at the end of your race.

PART III

MOMENTUM

18

METAMORPHOSIS

"Therefore, if anyone is in Christ, he is a new creation; the old has passed away, and see, the new has come!" (2 Corinthians 5:17 CSB)

To See

I was sitting next to Victoria, helping to support her arm so she could turn the page of a 3D book I had made for her. As I did this, she turned to look right at me. Right into my eyes. Three to five seconds passed as she gazed into my eyes. Time slowed down as I gazed right back into her beautiful liquid brown eyes. A true miracle.

Victoria was eight years old when she came to the United States from Bulgaria. Having been vastly undernourished from birth, she weighed a mere nine pounds upon arrival in Oregon. The first couple of years were spent getting her healthy. Among her complex conditions, Victoria was diagnosed with Wolf Hirschhorn Syndrome, cerebral palsy, and CVI. During the early days, she showed all the visual behaviors of a child in Phase I of the CVI Range. Very few functional visual behaviors were observed. Her eyes were open, but she had a blank stare, not looking at or processing anything, behaving as if blind. Eye contact with others was something the doctors said she would never be able to do, along with other things. Our team brainstormed how to help her become more mobile, more communicative, and more open to various sensory experiences. We wanted to explore ways to build more neural pathways and connections.

Having moved from Phase I to Phase II, Victoria, now sixteen years old, will scan around when entering a room demonstrating visual curiosity. She makes eye contact with us even when we are six feet away! Well beyond visual curiosity, Victoria has learned self advocacy. Within our time together we have created a structure that provides stable and familiar routines intertwined with the ability to make choices. Communication is supported through the use of her PODD book.

Smiles and vocalizations are more of a common behavior as Victoria realizes she is safe, has a voice, and is being listened to. What started as no communication, has now grown to a place where Victoria makes choices, shares how she feels, and tells us when she is done with something or wants to do something different. She has been given a voice and she is using it! After nearly seven years of work, progress and success are so gratifying. Metamorphosis is happening before our eyes. Truly a transformation!

To Be Seen

Dulce arrived from Mexico in 2022 with her mother and younger sister. She has cerebral palsy, is wheelchair-bound, non-verbal, and blind. The team I work with has spent hours getting to know Dulce and learning how she communicates. As we took time getting acquainted with her, we became aware of the way her body moved and slight nuances that most people would not notice. We started describing her body movements to her to shape her ability to say "yes" and "no." Gradually, she came to understand ways she could communicate with us. As we did with other students, we worked on using a PODD system with auditory partner assistance. This means the person who is sighted and verbal will read out various categories and choices within those categories for her to choose from. Dulce was getting her voice. She could choose between activities and share her feelings about something, either physical or emotional.

Dulce started high school this last year. I spent several days in her classroom training staff who had never worked with someone who was blind, non-verbal, and with limited mobility, on top of not speaking English. As I interacted with her while the staff observed, her personality came out. Dulce was smiling and laughing when doing preferred activities. When she was uncomfortable, Dulce demonstrated how she could make others aware a change in position was needed. With time and modeling, the staff no longer viewed her as someone they weren't sure what to do with but instead as someone of value. Dulce was being seen.

While Phase I shows little visual response, Phase II is characterized by visual responses increasing to the point where vision is now functional. Phase III displays the most visual behavior, almost like typical vision. As progression continues, the ability to see in one's environment increases. But CVI never goes away, and challenges will always exist. The challenges at this stage are mostly related to complexity, whether this be with an object, the background in which it is presented, or the busyness of the environment. An individual may do well in a quiet environment but have difficulty going to a fair or a concert. Visual fatigue is real, and taking a visual break is something that is needed throughout the day.

My ultimate goal when working with my students is not only that they develop their visual skills, but that they are given the ability to interact with the world around them to the fullest extent possible. In order to achieve this, there has to be a "buy-in" from all the people involved. This includes the teachers, the aides, the educational team, and the parents. When they observe me taking the time to work with my student and witness the student responding, the student moves from being unseen to being seen. Their value as a human being is brought to light.

Presumed competence refers to the belief that a person with a disability has the capacity to think, learn, and understand, even if tangible evidence isn't observed immediately. The amazing thing is, when we treat students this way, others observe this and are witness to the metamorphosis that occurs.

To Be Made New

A caterpillar transforming into a butterfly is one of the most straightforward symbols of metamorphosis. The process involved is quite amazing and is necessary for caterpillars to develop their wings. Hormones and the release of enzymes commence the dissolving of cells, muscles, the digestive system, and other organs inside the caterpillar. It becomes a liquid mess. But not everything inside the caterpillar is broken down.

Among all the changes that are occurring, specialized cells called *imaginal discs* come into play. They remain dormant until this time, but then these specialized cells start to wake up. Each of these discs contains a genetic recipe that targets a specific adult body part of the butterfly, starting from the inside out. During the first week, the digestive system is reformed. By day 16, the legs, wings, eyes, and mouth are all present and in working order. Each of these discs can have up to 50 cells that must be multiplied by the thousands precisely to form a specific part of the butterfly.

I think of the imaginal discs that are lying dormant in the caterpillar. Once specific hormones are elevated and specific enzymes are released, those imaginal discs come alive. They wake up.

I believe God works like that in each of us. We all are created with these imaginal discs waiting for His touch to "wake up." It's this yearning we have for more in life. This yearning ultimately leads us to Him, but it is our choice as to whether or not we will listen. The world tries to fill this yearning, this hole, with so many things that may appear good but take us away from God.

Metamorphosis is a messy process. It requires examining the filters we use to view life. It means dissolving those filters that are false and tell us lies about ourselves while acquiring filters that speak truth. It requires us to look at our past and deal with painful memories.

The thing is, we are not alone in this process. God is with us throughout, showing us He was with us all along and understands our pain, our grief. As we give it all to Him, transformation happens. We are given new wings. Wings that enable us to soar to new altitude, viewing life from His perspective.

To Look Outward

To see and to be seen. Both are important aspects of transformation.

We all have the opportunity to be made new. To have a new life. Like Victoria, we have been given the chance to be transformed. As the caterpillar's old body is done away with, so in the life of a person who comes to the Lord; the old dies away, leaving a new resurrected life. The old made new. New neural pathways replace old ones. Previous ways of thinking are dying. Our thoughts are now passing through new filters born out of God's truth and our rightful identity in Him. Transformation of our mind, of the way we think.

Even our outward appearance and how we present ourselves change. As we grow in intimacy with God, we learn to value ourselves, which in turn allows others to value us as well. Like Dulce, we begin to be seen by others for who we are in reality, people of value.

What is amazing is that a natural byproduct of being seen is the ability to now see others. To accurately see others through God's eyes. Throughout this book, we have focused on ways to see and be seen. To see ourselves are just the first steps. Once we grasp our identity, we naturally become missional in sharing God's love with those around us.

What is amazing is that a natural byproduct of being seen is the ability to now see others.

The book of Song of Songs in the Bible is about this process. The Passion Translation does an amazing job of demonstrating how God views us as His bride. How in love and delight He is with each of us. The last two chapters of this book show how the bride is now ready to share this love with others. This love is now reaching out to those around her. Inward to outward.

If we desire it and are willing to trust the process, to submit to God, we can move upward and forward into what God has prepared for us. It will be messy and painful at times, but it is how we earn our wings.

Will you step out and trust God to complete this process in you? I guarantee it will transform your life and the lives of those around you.

19

THE HOPE OF CHANGE

"Therefore if anyone is in Christ [this is, grafted in, joined to Him by faith in Him as Savior], he is a new creature [reborn and renewed by the Holy Spirit]; the old things [the previous moral and spiritual condition] have passed away. Behold, new things have come [because spiritual awakening brings a new life]." (2 Corinthians 5:17 AMP)

La Paz is a city that is shaped like a bowl. A valley that is surrounded by mountains. From the airport, which is on the altiplano (high plains of Bolivia), one main highway goes into the city. Until recently, due to the terrain of the earth with the presence of canyons throughout the city, it was challenging to build other main roadways. As a result, certain parts of the city could not connect to other parts. Even though they may be in close proximity, one would have to take the long way around to get to one's destination. Traffic jams were a constant reality, and it was often faster to walk somewhere then take the bus or ride a car.

The main highway of La Paz was like the visual pathway in the brain that goes from the eyes to the optic nerve through the thalamus to the visual cortex. With CVI, the main visual pathways are blocked and new pathways need to be created. Likewise, new modes of transportation needed to be constructed within La Paz to address the traffic problem.

In 2014, aerial cable cars were installed in the city and people are now able to get around much more easily. These new transportation routes have opened up more opportunities for people and made life much easier. Now, it may take only five to ten minutes to get to a nearby location, whereas before it would have taken more than an hour.

The Visual Process

As stated earlier, vision is a complex system occurring inside the brain. Information coming through the optic nerves from the eyes has to be cross-referenced with all other sensory input in order for the brain to make sense of what one is looking at. Vision isn't a single sensory event. It is a multi-sensory experience. As it is experienced, a memory is created. That memory is used as a reference for new information and new experiences occurring in the future. All these processes create neural pathways in the brain.

The brain is incredible in so many ways, but one amazing aspect of it is that it is always moldable. New neural pathways can be created at any time in our lives, both in the first visual pathway of the brain involving the thalamus where information is processed and relayed, and then in the pathways going beyond into the cerebral cortex where the interpretation of this information occurs.

The example of La Paz gives me hope. Hope in my own life that new routes can be formed in how I think, replacing false beliefs that have affected my life in unhealthy ways. Hope for my students as new routes and pathways are formed in their brains. In both my life and my students', new connections made possible for better sight, understanding, and interaction with our surroundings.

In order to aid in the creation of neural pathways, the thalamus needs to make sense of the visual information coming in through the optic nerves combined with other sensory input. Sensory-rich experiences are a crucial part of this process. The more sensory-rich experiences are provided, the more synaptic connections there will be, just like what happens with physical movement. The connections between the neurons will also become stronger as more senses are involved in an experience. There is a sensitive period for the first six or seven years of a person's life, but the brain continues to be moldable. These connections give rise to opportunities for a child to interact and experience, generating meaning and creating memories to continue building on.

Hope in Renewing Our Minds

Every summer, my daughter and I buy flowers to plant in big pots that are on our deck. Before we go buy, it is my job to get the soil ready in the pots. Because the pots are so huge, a lot of soil is in them and most of it is still good. I take out the old roots and the bad soil from the previous year and replace it with new soil, mixing it in to get ready for the new flowers.

This last year, I felt God tell me that He was going to walk with me through my erroneous filters and we would get rid of the "bad soil" together. This image brought so much peace and hope into my soul. Since then, possessing the knowledge of where these beliefs came from and where they started gave me the ability to stop partnering with them. Understanding that I did not have to believe them anymore was so freeing. That being said, it continues to be a process as those neural pathways that need to be replaced run deep.

Romans 12:2 tells us to "renew our minds." As I continue to learn about the brain, I have an increased understanding how this is what we are literally doing as we seek to become more and more like Jesus. An actual physical change occurs in our brains as we actively renew our minds. When you have a thought, neurons form. That thought pattern solidifies as neural connections increase. Change literally occurs at the cellular level with the way we think. It is important that the neurons that are forming be based on truth.

Building New Pathways Through Repetition

While it may seem impossible to change the way we think, especially if it is something we have inherited, hope is always present with God. I have a mug that states, "Impossible is God's starting point." Our God is the God of making the impossible possible. The majority of our thoughts are thoughts that we focus on over and over and over. This can be dangerous if our thoughts are not based on truth. If they are not in line with who God says we are. In order for our minds to be renewed, we need to be attentive to the lies we have bought into and understand they are not reality.

Neural pathways are created when repetition builds experiences that create meaning. For me, this renewal is happening day by day. Understanding how this happens physically, I began exploring ways to practice this. I began by using my 50 word gift in a new way. Some of my words from my box include "bold", "surrounded", "fearless", "held", "blessed", "healed".... I soak in these words and the corresponding verses. I randomly choose five words at the beginning of each day and take a picture of them with my phone. Throughout my day I go back and contemplate the meaning of these words and what they say about me in light of whatever situation I find myself in. By doing this, I am noticing my way of thinking is changing. More and more anxiety and fear are being replaced by confidence in who I am in Christ. Confidence that He is working through me. Confidence that I am protected in Him and He is providing for all I need. Peace and the expectation of God working are becoming more of the new normal for me.

It may be that for some, God speaks in a way we don't perceive. If there is no recognizable pattern already existing to anchor this incoming communication, the input may get discarded. It works much like the thalamus discarding sensory input that doesn't make sense because of the lack of connections in the brain. As we open ourselves to God, connections start to form, showing up in areas of our lives where God has been at work. We just didn't recognize it at the time. Our relationship with Him begins to grow. A relationship where when we pray for ourselves or someone else, we pray with expectancy recognizing God is at work because we have that anchor.

We are much more effective sharing God's love with others when we have a relationship that is already solid. Do you have enough of a spiritual foundation to recognize God at work in both yourself and others? Are you able to connect with the prior experiences of someone else to share God's love in a way they can understand?

Do you have enough of a spiritual foundation to recognize God at work in both yourself and others?

The Importance of Our Thoughts

What are practical ways you can begin to change your neural pathways and take hold of your true identity? Practical ways where you can take out the old soil and bring in new soil. Recognize the good soil that is present and plant more into this.

I encourage you to take some time and write down a list of what needs to be taken out. Read through the Bible and ask the Holy Spirit to show you thoughts and filters that do not resonate with what God says about you. Likewise, ask the Holy Spirit to bring to mind all that speaks truth to your life and who He says you are. Spend time sowing deeper into these truths. Start your own 50 word bank to draw from.

Many verses in the Bible address where to place our thoughts and how to direct our minds to think. It's this repetition and this building of neural pathways that takes intentionality and focus. Are you willing to take the time and energy to do this? It will change your life!

"You will keep in perfect peace all who trust in you, all whose *thoughts* are fixed on you!" (Isaiah 26:2 NLT, emphasis added).

"And now, dear brothers and sisters, one final thing. *Fix your thoughts* on what is true, and honorable, and right, and pure, and lovely, and admirable. Think about things that are excellent and worthy of praise" (Philippians 4:8 NLT, emphasis added).

"Don't copy the behavior and customs of this world, but let God transform you into a new person by *changing the way you think*" (Romans 12:2 NLT, emphasis added).

20

GLORY TO GLORY

"We all, with unveiled faces, are looking as in a mirror at the glory of the Lord and are being transformed into the same image from glory to glory; this is from the Lord who is the Spirit." (2 Corinthians 3:18 CSB)

My special greeting to Sydney is to place my hand on her leg by her knee, letting her become aware that I am beside her. After my greeting, we begin our time together.

One thing about Sydney is that she loves people. She has an older sister and a younger brother who both love to talk. They always have something to tell me. Sydney does not talk. She is nonverbal. Sydney is reaching the age of transitioning from early childhood services to entering the school system as a Kindergartener. An area of concern has been communication as she is deafblind along with limited motor ability. This concern extends to both how to communicate to Sydney as well as how to provide access for Sydney to be able to communicate with others.

It has been said that Speech-Language Pathologists (SLPs) and Alternative and Augmentative Communication (AAC) Specialists are the gatekeepers to communication. They have the keys that unlock the ability for an individual with complex needs to communicate. The decisions they make have a direct impact on how much a child will have a voice. This is a heavy responsibility to carry. It was Amy, both an SLP and AAC Specialist, who taught me the concept of presumed competence with each child I work with. To believe they have the capacity to communicate regardless of how little it may appear they do, both expressively and receptively at the time.

It is up to us to get to know the child and observe how they communicate and so adjust how we communicate with them. In so doing, we build a system accordingly that opens the door to communication for the child. It takes time and patience. It takes thinking outside the box and the willingness to try many things. It means realizing setbacks and failures will happen, but to keep trying. Each child has value and worth and deserves to have a voice and be heard, no matter how their disability presents itself.

Because deafblindness is such a low incidence disability, it is not always easy to find SLPs who understand how to work with these children. This last year with Sydney, we brought in a new team member who is one of the state specialists on deaf-blindness. Sydney's mom and I were amazed by this visit, with how much hope it brought that we could indeed build a communication system for Sydney.

Through this visit, it was made apparent how much Sydney does communicate already. When she is happy or excited, she will squeal and bring her arms up. When Sydney is uncomfortable, she will push her feet down and move her head from side to side. To show her awareness of other people, she will turn her head towards them. We have since started building Sydney's own unique dictionary. This dictionary will travel with her and give others direction in how to communicate with her as well as how to respond to the way she communicates. Through this dictionary, she will be listened to and understood! There is hope that her voice will be given an outlet and she will be able to interact with those around her.

An Unveiled Face

One of my favorite themes in movies and books is people being transformed through hardship. I love stories about people overcoming difficulties and persevering, whether these be physical or emotional.

As a teacher, I love watching my students blossom and come into their own, and to have others' perception of them change. To see them no longer regarded as a victim or needy or swallowed up by the environment. To be witness to watching this awareness come into play, both coming from the student as well as those around them. Recognition dawning that they have an impact in the world.

Sydney is in the process of both learning to see and to be seen by others. As she is learning to see, the cells are firing in her brain, making connections and building new pathways. Renewal and transformation are taking place.

Likewise, we are being transformed from the inside out through the renewing of our minds. The more we turn to Jesus and gaze upon Him, the more we become like Him. We are being transformed into His image. Can you imagine looking into the mirror and seeing Him looking back at you through your reflection?

In Exodus when Moses was leading the Israelites out of Egypt and they were living in the desert, he would meet with God. After these times, he had to wear a veil over his face because the people couldn't look at him; God's glory shone through him (see Exodus 34). God removed this veil when He sent His son Jesus to die and bear our sin upon the cross. What a demonstration of His love and desire for a relationship with us. No more barriers.

To be able to look at Jesus with an *unveiled* face. In the original language this passage was written in, the word means "unhidden" or "uncovered" (see 2 Corinthians 2:18). So to be able to look upon Jesus with an *unveiled* face is to focus with a clear gaze where nothing is hidden or blurry. To be able to focus where nothing is in the way to prevent one from seeing clearly. All filters muddied with sin and lies gone, replaced by His face. This isn't done through physical eyes but through our inner person. Like Sydney learning to see and communicate through additional means besides her eyes, we are learning to see Jesus through all our sensory channels. Our own communication with Him is expanding in the process.

Our part is to turn and choose to look upon His face. In His incredible love, God gives us free will. He wants us to want Him and for this to be our choice. As we choose to focus on Him, to gaze upon His face, transformation occurs. His thoughts become our thoughts. His desires, our desires. We begin to look more and more like Him, reflecting His face as our own as though looking at oneself in a mirror.

The Act of Transformation

As mentioned earlier, one of my favorite pastimes is hunting for agates along the Oregon coast. At first glance, no agates can be seen, but as I spend time digging and peering closely on the ground, agates are found. As a deep thinker, I find myself regarding these broken pieces of rock that hold so much beauty and equating them to what the world may perceive as "broken" but in reality have so much beauty. In a way it reminds me of what it's like discovering my student has a voice, something not previously recognized.

In order to find the most beautiful agates, you have to get near the ground and brush past the surface layer of rocks to go deeper. Likewise, you have to get close to your student, investing time, becoming familiar with who they are and their movements. It's bringing to light those subtle movements that convey understanding and the dawning recognition from the student the first time they grasp what you have been trying to communicate.

In order to find the most beautiful agates, you have to get near the ground and brush past the surface layer of rocks to go deeper.

It is a beautiful process, this witnessing of someone discovering their voice. It brings me to tears every time and makes all the hard work and time worth it. To watch them realize they have a "say so" in their life and when they communicate it impacts those around them. Life changing. Worth and value brought to the forefront. This is what it means to see and be seen, to hear and be heard! This is to all the Henrys, Dulces, Victorias, and Sydneys that I have met and worked with over the years. You make the world a better place, and my life is better because of you! You are all agates in my life.

I imagine this is a bit of what God experiences when we choose to look at Him. When we choose to have a relationship with Him and give Him all our hurts. When we allow healing to penetrate our deepest wounds. If the amount of joy and pleasure I feel watching even the smallest transformation in my students is any basis of measurement, how much more God must feel when He watches us realize our true identity in Him! Our true value and worth. I don't believe anything else gives the Father greater joy than this.

Glory to Glory

I used to sing the song "Glory to Glory," not understanding what it was about. Now I understand this more and am aware of how God works in us. I love watching in my mind all those neural connections and pathways being formed as I spend time in God's presence getting to know Him. There is always more to learn, more areas to grow in.

All a part of His glory.

Through this never ending increase of glory, we increase in our ability to change the world. To make an impact on those around us as well as those who we may never meet. We are in continual transformation, living in the process of becoming who we were created to be.

Going from glory to glory... I used to wonder what this meant. Now I have an idea. I am beginning to get it.

Every one of these glories, an agate:

Moving through life feeling more alive than I have ever felt before. Experiencing God's presence beside me and having this expectation of Him working in whatever situation I find myself in. Glory to glory.

Jon looking back and experiencing the faithfulness of God in his job as the president of the teachers union in our town despite all the challenges. Glory to glory.

Watching Reilly grow in his giftings in music, already making a difference in the world and sharing his love of God. Glory to glory.

Witnessing Paige discover God in her own journey. Going from not being certain she believed in God to being passionate about following Him. Glory to glory.

Watching Peter overcome his fear of new things and discover joy. Glory to glory.

Having the honor of walking alongside good friends as they work through incredible trauma in their lives and being a first-hand witness of God's healing and bringing redemption to their separate circumstances. Glory to glory.

Being witness to the transformation happening in the Henrys, Dulces, Victorias, and Sydneys in my life. Watching them discover their voices and that they have value. That is true vision. Glory to glory.

Seeing my prayers over the years being answered of having deep friendships with other women who encourage and sharpen me in my faith. My cup truly overflows. Glory to glory.

Praying for someone and witnessing the healing take place. My faith blossoming. Glory to glory.

Confronting my own fears in faith that God will take care of me, and experiencing His provision and protection every single time. Glory to glory.

Waking up in the middle of the night to walk around my home, praying for each member. Noticing the changes happen and the difference prayer makes. Glory to glory.

Playing the piano in His presence, not realizing hours have passed. Glory to glory.

Realizing that my responses to situations are becoming more Holy Spirit influenced. Instead of having reactions involving fear, anxiety, and anger, my reactions are characterized by peace, compassion, and patience. I am being transformed to become more like Jesus. Glory to glory.

Glory to glory. What are your glory to glory agates? You may have more than you realize. God is working.

CONCLUSION

TO SEE AND BE SEEN—TO KNOW AND BE KNOWN

Life has a way of throwing us curveballs. As I have been finishing this book, our family home was hit by more than eight trees during a series of ice storms in Springfield. Spikes from 80-foot Douglas Firs pierced our home in several rooms, making the house uninhabitable. Thankfully, they missed us as my son Peter and I were inside the house while my husband Jon watched the first tree fall from the outside. We moved out, wondering if our house would be salvageable or not. It was traumatic, but with God already working through the situation demonstrating to me and my family, we are both seen and known by Him.

Throughout this last experience, I have noticed a deep peace, knowing I'm being taken care of. It proves my neural pathways have indeed changed and have been rerouted away from the fear of being forgotten. We've received so much support from family, friends, and colleagues. As the insurance adjusters were walking through our house, I found myself chuckling inside, wondering what they thought as they saw our plaques on the walls, one with the word "Blessed" and another with Psalm 46:10: "Be still and know that I am God." To them it may not have seemed congruent with the situation, but as I read those words, I genuinely felt their truth. I was blessed in the midst of all this unexpected chaos and trauma with the deep awareness that God was in control.

Like my grandparents, Jon and I always imagined we would raise our family overseas, although not necessarily as missionaries. We spent four years experiencing life in three different countries early in our marriage with the intention of settling down in one of these countries long-term as teachers. But we were thrown a curveball—our boys were born with disabilities and our plans changed.

Most of the parents of the students I work with were also thrown a curveball when they learned of their child's disability along with the impact of this disability. I now view my experience as a blessing as I can relate to the families I work with because I have gone through the same experience. Through the challenge of my sons' disabilities, my life was redirected from being a classroom teacher to becoming a Teacher for the Visually Impaired. I focused in the area of visual impairment, in particular, CVI. I delved deep into the process of vision in the brain. I sensed that to indeed be effective with my students and provide intervention that had results, I needed to understand how vision works.

I find it so amazing how this focus on CVI correlates strongly with my desire from a young age to care for those who are alone, starting with all those sticks, stones, and leaves. Throughout my life, I have continued to be drawn to those who are left out, or forgotten. In the early years of my career, students with this type of visual impairment seemed to fall through the cracks. This was due largely to being a diagnosis that is relatively new and has been misunderstood. Learning about CVI has become my passion, along with training others. What kept being brought to my attention was that as I studied how vision happens in the brain, I saw more and more correlations between what I was learning and my own walk with God. I began to further understand how incredibly He has imprinted His image on each one of us. God knows me so thoroughly. He brought together my passion for others to coincide with my passion for Him in a way that continually amazes me. I am truly seen by Him.

What is compelling about these curveball stories is that in the midst of changed plans, unexpected blessings were discovered. No one ever plans for a natural disaster to occur, potentially destroying their house. We are still waiting to find out the extent of damage and figuring out where we will be living. No one ever plans to have a child with a disability. Like all the families I work with, our plans changed. What is amazing is how God showed Himself present from the beginning, and we were able to recognize the unexpected blessings, the agates. Families and friends stepped up to take care of us through it all. More countless agates.

Living in Expectation

This last year, I gifted my dad with a sign that says, "Live expectantly". It's a reminder to live in expectation everyday, knowing that God is working. Expectation that He will provide for our needs. Expectation that He will go beyond what we imagine or think to bless us. Expectation that He indeed sees us, knows us, and will act accordingly in ways that bring us closer to Him. Expectation that throughout our past, present, and future, He can use all the curveballs and surprises life may throw at us. Nothing is too difficult for Him. And if we are paying attention, we will find He does so in such a way that shows how much He sees us, knows us, loves us.

This theme of being seen and known, started burning inside of me a couple years ago. This desire to want to be known was deep. To be seen for who I am by others. But I feared that if others really knew me, I might not be accepted with all my quirks and insecurities.

My son Reilly and I had a recent conversation about what all humanity yearns for. It boils down to two things: to be known and to be loved. With this comes the two things people fear most: to not be known, or to be known and not loved.

We all yearn to be known for who we are and still be loved unreservedly and unconditionally. I don't know if this is possible with appearance but at the heart. His heart is for those who feel forgotten. He is drawn to those who have been set aside by society and deemed of little value. If you identify with this latter category as I once did, take courage! God sees you! God knows you! God loves you!

Because God sees you and loves you, He enables you to see yourself as the person He created you to be. This in turn, leads you to see, know, and love others.

ABOUT THE AUTHOR

As a child, Kristin Gault knew that when she grew up, she wanted to help people. Raised in Bolivia, the daughter of missionary parents, she experienced first-hand the needs of people often forgotten in their own context. Her relationship to Jesus, beginning in childhood and growing through adulthood, strengthened the commitment of reaching out to others.

Back home in the US, Kristin completed her bachelor's degree in sociology/social work, thinking this might open doors to work with people. But as she and her husband Jon lived overseas the first four years of their marriage, she discovered how much she loved teaching. She went back to school to get a degree in elementary education and then taught a blended 4th/5th grade classroom for five years. During this time, her own children were born. The diagnosis of her two sons, Reilly and Peter, with visual impairments propelled her back to school for a second masters degree that would enable her to become a Teacher for the Visually Impaired (TVI).

Kristin has been a TVI in Oregon since 2012. She has specialized training in cortical/cerebral visual impairment (CVI) and provides assessments, interventions, and strategies for students with this condition throughout Lane County. Beyond her TVI role, Kristin is a member of the statewide Oregon CVI Team and has run trainings throughout the Pacific Northwest both with a team and on her own. Kristin's hands-on experience and research inspired her to create VistaQuest and its intervention tool, the BaseKit, geared especially for students with CVI. This tool is now being used throughout the United States and is spreading to other countries.

Kristin and her husband Jonathan are parents to three amazing children, two who are now adults and one in high school. Being a parent to two sons with disabilities has given Kristin the ability to connect with the families that she works with. She understands their unique challenges and the need to advocate for one's child. She understands the importance of making sure her daughter, who does not have a disability, is also seen and heard.

Kristin has a BA in sociology/social work from George Fox University (1995) and M.Ed in elementary education from Pacific University (2001), an MA in becoming a Teacher for the Visually Impaired from University of Northern Colorado (2012), and specialized training in CVI from Perkins University (throughout career as a TVI).

She currently participates in the Thrive Community Church in Eugene, Oregon.

VISTAQUEST™

Going Deeper

Cortical/cerebral visual impairment is now the leading cause of visual impairment in the world. It is one of the least understood visual impairments as well as being vastly undiagnosed. It is believed that there is one student out of every thirty who have undiagnosed CVI. This book addresses only part of the process of how vision occurs. For those who want to go deeper on this subject of vision, here are some resources:

VistaQuest.org

Facebook: VistaQuest

Instagram: _VistaQuest

Email: kristin@vistaquest.org

ACKNOWLEDGMENTS

First of all, I want to thank my husband, Jonathan. You have been a rock for me and our family throughout the years. Whenever challenges come and life plans change, you have stood firm. You show me how to trust and believe God is going to take care of us. I love you and couldn't have asked for a better partner in life.

To Reilly, Paige, and Peter: I couldn't imagine life without you. Being your mom has absolutely been one of the greatest joys of my life. You have challenged me to grow in ways I never imagined possible. Your support for all I have done and am doing is something I don't take lightly. They say that a parent's ceiling is the foundation for their kids. I am already amazed by what God is doing in your lives and the vision of what God will continue to do. He is faithful and will do more than what you could ever imagine. Just keep your eyes on Him.

To my parents, Hal and Nancy Thomas: thank you for the way you raised David and me. Through your love and guidance we were able to observe firsthand what a personal close relationship with the Lord looks like. I look up to you both and am proud to be your daughter.

To my brother, David: I love how you have always supported me. I value our friendship and all our shared memories. I could not have asked for a more awesome big brother!

To Anita: you are my greatest cheerleader. Words can't even describe how much I love you. Starting from when I came back from Bolivia to the present, you always seem to know how to support me. You have always believed in me when I didn't believe in myself. You have no idea how your phone calls, from wherever you were in the world at that time, would lift me up when I was at my lowest. Our times together during summers when you visit Oregon are always a highlight. I will always treasure our celebratory 50th birthday triathlon!

To my Thursday group, or Andi's group, as I also call it: Andi, Marie, Colleen, Betsy, Celeste, Jill, Patty, Heather, and Sherri (even though you live far away, your words and openness to the Holy Spirit have had such an impact on me). We have been through so much together and I value every second of it. Thank you for providing a safe environment where I could grow. I feel seen and known by each one of you, and our times spent together has enabled much healing to occur.

To Deb, Jess, and Amanda: Your friendship means the world to me and is something I treasure deeply. The way each of you has inspired and challenged me has brought me closer to Him. You have gifted me with another safe place to be seen and known. The impact you have each had on my life has changed me for the better!

To my Bolivian family and friends: *Humberto y Petrona, Noemí and Dina —ustedes son mis tíos y hermanas de sangre. Siempre van a tener un lugar muy especial en mi corazón; Mariela, otra amiga de mi niñez—aunque no nos vemos mucho, tu amistad y todas las memorias que tenemos me dan mucha alegría; Ana María, Ercilia, David Q., Abraham, y David Y.—tenemos una gran historia y tantas memorias de tiempos que hemos compartido. Siempre van a tener un lugar especial en mi corazón.* Craig—you were the bright spot in my life at the American Cooperative School.

To my extended family, including all my incredible aunts, uncles, cousins, nieces, and nephews: You all bring so much joy and expertise in where God has placed you. Don't ever doubt your worth! Bree, I treasure our times together and love discovering how alike we are. I have learned so much from your area of expertise as well as from you, Mark and Chelsea!

To Soorin Backer and her ministry: All those conferences I have attended and the many Friday nights spent at OARS have truly changed me as I have experienced God's love for me over and over again through these times.

To my colleagues and the ICAN (Individuals with Complex Access Needs) team: I have learned so much through each of you. Barbara, your sacrifice of time and doing photo shoots together showing Paige her beauty, inside and out, has been priceless. I so appreciate your wisdom from your own years of working with students who are blind and visually impaired, and value it along with your friendship. Amy, I absolutely love working with you! The way you value each child demonstrating presumed competence has changed the way I teach. It has shown me what is most important in my job. I love my ICAN team as I have learned from each one of you so much. Thank you for the time and effort you put into our students.

To three women who have helped me believe in myself: Saaron, thank you for all the time and support you have given me as we have delved into the world of CVI together. I look forward to continuing to learn together. CJ, thank you for leading me into forming and beginning VistaQuest. I love how you jumped into learning about something so new to you, and then grasped the importance and value of it. You always knew when to push me beyond my comfort zone while giving the right amount of support. I couldn't have done it without you! Heather, your friendship this last year has been such a blessing! You have also helped push me out of my comfort zone and helped me believe in myself.

To all the parents and families of my students: you are some of the most courageous people I know! The daily challenges you face and the way you live your life that no one else can see, yet you continue to step up. You are my biggest heroes, who I look up to. This goes to you: Lauren, Lindsay, Karissa, Maria, Ashley, Laurie, Emily, Hallie, and many others.

To Jonathan and Natalie: Both of you speak life to me. Jonathan, you planted the seed last year telling me I should write a book when the thought had never crossed my mind.

anyone except Jesus. No other religion exists where we can be so thoroughly known and loved. Only through Jesus.

We all have areas in our lives that we do not entirely understand. Relationships where we have the best of intentions but where we act in a way we do not want to. Situations that trigger us and we don't understand why. We aren't given the full picture of all that is going on in our lives. But we can rest in the knowledge that God does. Right now. I am convinced God knows us completely. He understands how we think and why we think the way we do. He formed our personalities and we are created in His image. He understands us. It all comes down to trust. Trust that He is taking care of us and our needs. Trust that He has full awareness of the mistakes we make along the way and is able to use those mistakes and turn them around for His glory in spite of ourselves. A day will come when we will be able to behold the whole picture.

In the meantime, I believe God has a way of using every situation and circumstance in our lives to bring us to greater awareness of Him. A greater awareness of how much He loves us, cares for us, and desires an intimate relationship with each one of us. We just have to be willing and open to Him. It is easy to want to blame God for when bad things happen, especially when they are beyond our power or ability to influence. We cannot control what others do, and we often get hurt through the selfish actions of others. We also get hurt through events that no one has command over like sickness and disease or natural disasters. God is all powerful, so it is easy to assume He can stop bad things from happening. But in His love, He gifts us with free will because He wants us to come to Him on our own accord. With that free will, we have the ability to make choices that can either hurt or help us. Our reaction and these choices we make when bad things happen to us are what we can control. Choices that will either bring us closer to Him or further away.

Our human definition of what holds value is so different from what God values. People tend to value pleasure, power, fame, wealth, ability, strength, and pride. God, on the other hand, values humility, servanthood, and meekness. He doesn't look at the outward

To all my beta readers Mom/Nancy, Deb, Andi, Celeste, Lauren, Sooren, Lindsay: your feedback and the time you took to read this is something I highly value and appreciate!

And last, but not least, to Jesse and Elisheba: I could not have done this without you. A year ago I had no idea I was going to write a book. You both have been with me every step of the way. Offering guidance through prayer and encouragement. When I got stuck and wondered if I had anything worth sharing, you both convinced me otherwise. I am thankful from the bottom of my heart!